7X 10/07

D0100013

L I F E W A Y S

The Nez Perce

R A Y M O N D   B I A L

Benchmark Books

MARSHALL CAVENDISH
NEW YORK

SERIES CONSULTANT: JOHN BIERHORST

ACKNOWLEDGMENTS

The Nez Perce would not have been possible without the assistance of several organizations and individuals, who have committed themselves to preserving the traditions of the Nez Perce. I am especially indebted to the National Park Service for helpful advice and permission to photograph along the Nez Perce National Historic Trail. I would also like to thank the National Archives, the Library of Congress, and the Philbrook Museum of Art for furnishing a number of fine illustrations.

I would like to acknowledge my editors Kate Nunn and Doug Sanders for their many valuable suggestions regarding this book and other titles in the Lifeways series. I would like to thank John Bierhorst for his expert review of the manuscript. As always, I reserve my deepest regard for my wife, Linda, and my children Anna, Sarah, and Luke, who have always been my inspiration.

Benchmarks Books
Marshall Cavendish Corporation
99 White Plains Road, Tarrytown, New York 10591-9001
Text copyright © 2002 by Raymond Bial
Map copyright © 2002 by the Marshall Cavendish Corporation
Map by Rodica Prato

Library of Congress Cataloging-in-Publication Data
Bial, Raymond.
The Nez Perce / Raymond Bial.
p. cm. — (Lifeways)
Includes bibliographical references and index.
ISBN 0-7614-1210-7
1. Nez Perce Indians—Juvenile literature. [1. Nez Perce Indians.
2. Indians of North America—Northwest, Pacific.] I. Title.
E99.N5 B45 2002   979.5004'9741—dc21   00-059627
Printed in Italy
6 5 4 3 2

Photo Research by Candlepants Incorporated

Cover Photo: Ray Bial

The photographs in this book are used by permission and through the courtesy of; Northwest Museum of Art and Culture: Photo #L93-72.52, 1, Photo #L93-72.109, 29, Photo #L94-53.167, 48, Photo #L94-7.105, 53, Photo #L97-18.1, 72, Photo #L94-53.30, 77, #L93-72.31, 84-85. Raymond Bial, 6, 8-9, 10, 13, 16, 25, 26-27, 31, 36, 39, 42-43, 45, 51, 54, 58, 61, 63, 64, 66, 68-69, 71, 79, 81, 98-99, 101, 102-103. Idaho Historical Society: Photo #63-221.18, 20. Special Collections Divisions, University of Washington Libraries: Photo #NA940, 32, Photo #NA1026, 47, Photo #NA1294, 74-75, Photo #NA1285, 88, Photo #NA4169, 91, Photo # NA604, 109, Photo #NA605, 111, Photo #NA627, 113, Photo #NA878, 114. National Anthropological Archives: Photo #2977, 35, 107. Tony Esparza/CBS: 112.

This book is respectfully dedicated
to the Nez Perce.

Contents

1.Origins 8

"Coyote and the Monster" • The People and the Land

2.Camps and Villages 26

Pit Houses and Other Dwellings • Appaloosa Horses

3.Lifeways 42

Cycle of Life • Warfare • Hunting, Fishing, and Gathering • Recipe: Elk Stew • Clothing and Jewelry • Handicrafts

4.Beliefs   68
Rites and Ceremonies • Games • "The Salmon and the Five Swallow Sisters"

5.Changing World   84
Nez Perce Language

6.New Ways   98

More About the Nez Perce   102
Time Line • Notable People • Glossary • Further Information

Index   125

Author's Note

AT THE DAWN OF THE TWENTIETH CENTURY, NATIVE Americans were thought to be a vanishing race. However, despite four hundred years of warfare, deprivation, and disease, American Indians have not gone away. Countless thousands have lost their lives, but over the course of this century the populations of native tribes have grown tremendously. Even as American Indians struggle to adapt to modern Western life, they have also kept the flame of their traditions alive—the language, religion, stories, and the everyday ways of life. An exhilarating renaissance in Native American culture is now sweeping the nation from coast to coast.

The Lifeways books depict the social and cultural life of the major nations, from the early history of native peoples in North America to their present-day struggles for survival and dignity. Historical and contemporary photographs of traditional subjects, as well as period illustrations, are blended throughout each book so that readers may gain a sense of family life in a tipi, a hogan, or a longhouse.

No single book can comprehensively portray the intricate and varied lifeways of an entire tribe, or nation. I only hope that young people will come away with a deeper appreciation for the rich tapestry of Indian culture—both then and now—and a keen desire to learn more about these first Americans.

1. Origins

Rivers wind their way
through the rolling hills of
the ancestral homeland of
the Nez Perce.

MANY TALES OF THE NEZ PERCE (NEZ PURSE) TELL HOW COYOTE FORMED the land. The rock arch known as Ant and Yellow Jacket recalls the story of these once-friendly insects. When Ant spotted Yellow Jacket sitting on *his* rock, contently eating a piece of dried salmon, he told his friend he should have asked permission before taking the seat. Tempers flared as, rearing back on their hind legs, the two insects became locked in combat. Coyote passed by and demanded that they stop fighting. When they refused, Coyote turned them into stone.

In another story, associated with a landmark known as Coyote's Fishnet, Coyote was fishing with a huge net in Clearwater River. One day, Black Bear came by and asked Coyote why he was fishing instead

Ant and Yellowjacket, a rock formation nine miles east of Lewiston, Idaho, symbolizes the battling insects in the time-honored Nez Perce story.

of buffalo hunting with his people. Coyote became red-faced when he realized that he had simply forgotten to go on the hunt. Black Bear teased Coyote for his negligence. Aggravated by the taunts, Coyote flung his large fishnet over the river, caught Black Bear, and hurled him up the hillside where he remains as a stone figure.

Just east of Kamiah, Idaho, not far from the Clearwater River, there is a large rock formation known to the Nez Perce as Heart of the Monster. In ancestral stories, this landmark is all that is left of a cruel giant slain by Coyote. The rock formation also marks where the Nez Perce crossed the Clearwater River when they had to leave their homeland, which they had lost during the war of 1877. Moreover, the story of the great monster tells how the Nez Perce themselves had been put on Earth by Coyote.

Coyote and the Monster

Many years ago, while Coyote was visiting some friends on the Yakima River, a fierce and ugly monster dropped from the sky. With great noise and confusion he landed in Kamiah Valley. Covered with scales, the Monster snorted hot blasts of air that scorched the trees and grass. With his foul breath, he sucked the creatures of the valley into his huge, red mouth and swallowed them whole.

The Monster's appetite was so great that he devoured most of the animals. Only a few small creatures, such as Hummingbird, were able to flee to the mountains.

When Hummingbird met Coyote, he told him, "There is a horrible monster at Kamiah Valley who has eaten all the animals."

"Even the large animals?" Coyote asked in alarm.

Hummingbird explained, "I escaped only because I am so little. He has even devoured Rattlesnake, Grizzly Bear, and Black Bear."

"I will return to my people and try to help them," Coyote said, "but I must be very careful."

On the way to Kamiah Valley, Coyote gathered a bundle of sticks from a pine tree. He made ten sharp flint knives and a bow and many arrows, and gathered camas roots and couse, or biscuitroot, plants. Before approaching the Monster, he prepared for battle by painting himself with blue clay. He then drew near, tied himself to the mountain with tough, wild grapevines, and shouted, "Here I am, Monster!"

The Monster squinted with beady eyes, but, because he was nearly blind, he could not spot Coyote. "That must be Coyote," the Monster thought. "He is the only large animal I haven't swallowed. However, I must be careful, because Coyote is very clever."

"You're a great one!" Coyote mocked. "You can't even see me, and I'm in plain sight."

"But I can still eat you!" the Monster roared like distant thunder rolling over the mountains.

"Just try to inhale me with your hot, smelly breath," Coyote taunted.

Suspecting that Coyote meant to trick him, the Monster pronounced, "No, you have the greatest magic and medicine of all the animals. You try to draw me into your mouth with your breath."

*L*ocated in East Kamiah, Idaho, near an historic Nez Perce crossing point along the Clearwater River, Heart of the Monster is another landmark that has found its way into the stories of the tribe.

"Get ready," Coyote told him, and he drew powerful breaths, one after another. The Monster trembled and shook, but Coyote could not budge the gigantic body.

"Ha!" the Monster cried. "You cannot move me, and now I will devour you."

The Monster drew such a powerful breath that, despite the grape-vines, Coyote was nearly torn from the mountain. The force was so strong and so painful that Coyote had to cut himself loose. Waiting for just the right moment to sever the grapevines, he shot through the air over the broad prairie between the Salmon River and the Kamiah Valley. While flying over this land, he scattered camas roots and couse plants, saying, "This will be the best place for digging camas and couse. Future generations will come here and enjoy bountiful harvests." And today the plants grow thick there, amid streams of cool water and shady groves.

But Coyote was not out of danger. As if swept up in the winds of a powerful storm, he sailed toward the gaping red mouth of the Monster.

"At last I've got you!" the Monster howled triumphantly. "I will gobble you as I did the other miserable animals!"

Caught in the hot stench of the Monster's powerful breath, Coyote flew into the mouth and down the throat into the bottom of the ugly beast's stomach. In the dim light, he found all the other animals.

Striking at Coyote with his fangs, Rattlesnake angrily reproached him, "Why didn't you kill the Monster and save us? You are no great hero. You've been eaten, just like us!"

Nimbly jumping aside, Coyote asked, "Why do you wish to bite me? You could help yourself a little by biting the Monster instead." He then stepped on Rattlesnake's head, which is why it is flat.

Grizzly Bear chided Coyote, "Some leader you are, letting an important creature like me be swallowed by the Monster."

Coyote was so angry that he struck the lumbering animal on the nose, leaving a little dent, which Grizzly Bear still carries between his eyes.

Coyote next came upon Black Bear who was crying, "I'm afraid I'm going to die in here."

"Don't be silly," Coyote answered, and he twisted Black Bear's nose, which is why this creature's face looks so comical.

Coyote observed that all the animals were sad and hungry. Why should they starve, he asked himself, when the Monster has such a big heart surrounded with gobs of fat. So, with the pine sticks, he built a fire under the heart and soon the Monster was groaning in pain from the blistering heat. Coyote then began to cut away at the heart with one of the flint knives. But the flesh was so tough that several of the knives broke, one after another.

The Monster was now bellowing in agony, "Coyote is burning my insides and cutting my heart out. Why didn't I simply leave him alone?"

The fire had cooked the fat, and the animals gathered around for a great feast while Coyote continued to hack at the heart with the remaining knives. Finally, he cut the heart loose. The Monster staggered to the ground and died. When the animals had eaten their fill,

*T*hese forested slopes overlook the Heart of the Monster rock formation. It was from trees such as these that Coyote gathered pine sticks in preparation for his battle with the Monster.

they hurried out of the dead body—some through the mouth, others through the ears and nostrils. Everyone escaped without injury, except Muskrat whose tail was caught in the Monster's teeth. Muskrat nevertheless pulled his tail through, scraping off the hair, which is why the rodent now has a flat, naked tail.

Cottontail jumped for joy when she saw the bright sunshine, and Bald Eagle soared high into the blue sky. Everyone rejoiced and thanked Coyote who accepted their praise with modesty. But what should they do with the enormous body of the Monster?

Wise Coyote thought long and hard. Finally, he took the last flint knife and cut up Monster's body, making a large heap of bones and another of strips of flesh. He gazed with dismay upon the two piles. "This will never do," he said. "Generations of people are coming here. There will not be room for them."

So, he flung the thigh bones far over the Sawtooth Mountains, and the Blackfeet, a tall, long-legged people, came to live there. He threw the fat over the Rocky Mountains to the land of the Sioux, whom Coyote predicted would be a stocky people. He tossed the wide ribs to the land of the Flatheads who became broad-shouldered. He scattered the flesh and bones to all the places where people came to make their homes, including the Cheyenne, Crow, Yakima, Spokane, and many others.

When he was done, Fox pointed out, "You have forgotten the people who will live here, Coyote."

"I did forget that tribe," Coyote gasped. "But I still have some of the Monster's blood on my hands. I will sprinkle the drops over this land. There will be a people here. It will not be a large tribe, but they will have the bravest warriors on earth."

And so the Nimipu, or Nez Perce, came to live in the valley. And all that is left of the Monster is his burned heart, which has long since turned to stone. If you go to Kamiah Valley, you can see this rock formation in an open field, evidence of Coyote's wise and courageous deed.

LIKE THE OTHER NATIVE PEOPLES OF NORTH AMERICA, THE ANCESTORS OF the Nez Perce originally migrated from Siberia thousands of years ago, possibly crossing the Bering Strait over a slender land bridge that once connected Asia and Alaska or traveling in boats close to the shore. Hunters and gatherers, they eventually made their homes in villages along the rivers and in the valleys of what became the American Northwest. While the women gathered roots, berries, and seeds, the men hunted in the forests and fished in the cold, clear streams. When fish and game in their immediate area became scarce, the Nez Perce moved and established another village.

Members of the Sahaptian language family, the Nez Perce are also known as the Sahaptins. They call themselves *Nimipu* or *Nimapu*, meaning "real people." The name Nez Perce, originally Nez Percé (nay per SAY), which means "pierced nose," came from early French fur traders who were actually referring to several tribes in the Northwest who pierced their noses. One of the largest and most powerful of the various tribes in the region, the Nez Perce dominated a vast stretch of territory along the Clearwater and Snake Rivers in what is now western Idaho, northeastern Oregon, and southeastern Washington. For hundreds of years, the Nez Perce lived in settled villages, migrating seasonally as they hunted, fished, and gathered plants.

Initially, the Nez Perce lived in pit houses which they covered with branches and soil. However, when they acquired horses in the early 1700s they began to adopt a lifestyle similar to that of the Sioux, Cheyenne, and other inhabitants of the plains. The sheltered grasslands in their home country allowed the Nez Perce to raise some of the largest and finest herds of horses in North America. Expert breeders and trainers, they have become famous for the fast and sturdy horse with spotted markings known as the Appaloosa. Riding their impressive mounts, they expanded their trade with neighboring tribes—on both the Great Plains and the Pacific Coast. They also began to make yearly trips to the sprawling prairie to hunt buffalo. They adorned their clothes in increasingly lavish ways and began to live in tipis (TEE peez), like those of Plains Indians.

The Nez Perce favored a loose tribal organization in which the chief of each band served as the voice for his followers. When confronted with a major challenge, such as a conflict with another tribe, the chiefs gathered in council with respected medicine men, elders, and war chiefs. The Nez Perce enjoyed friendly relations with most of the other tribes in the Plateau region, including the Walla Walla, Yakima, Palouse, and Cayuse. They warred primarily with Plains tribes such as the Shoshone, North Paiute, and Bannock. However, each summer they called a truce with these tribes so they could trade with them.

Skilled horse trainers and riders, the Nez Perce were able to travel great distances to trade with other Native Americans and to hunt buffalo as well.

In 1805, the Nez Perce encountered the explorers Meriwether Lewis and William Clark at Weippe Prairie when their expedition passed through the Wallowa Valley in Idaho. The Nez Perce offered food and shelter to the cold, exhausted, and hungry party. After the explorers had rested, the Nez Perce helped them construct boats and guided them for the remainder of their journey to the Pacific Coast. Over the next several decades, the Nez Perce established friendly relations with both French-Canadian and American fur traders, as well as missionaries and settlers who entered their territory. As more settlers moved into the Northwest, other tribes went to war to save their lands. But the Nez Perce were able to avoid conflicts. By the mid-1800s, however, the Nez Perce were nonetheless forced from their lands and placed on reservations—but not without a fight that became one of the most remarkable acts of courage in the history of Indian resistance.

The People and the Land

"This country holds your father's body. Never sell the bones
of your father and your mother."—Old Joseph

Nez Perce territory was in the Plateau region of western North America, a vast and varied expanse between the Cascade Range and the Rocky Mountains in what is now Idaho and adjoining parts of eastern Washington and Oregon. In ancient times, the Plateau was covered by lava from volcanoes. This region of mountain ridges and softly rolling hills is marked by deep canyons and ravines cut in the

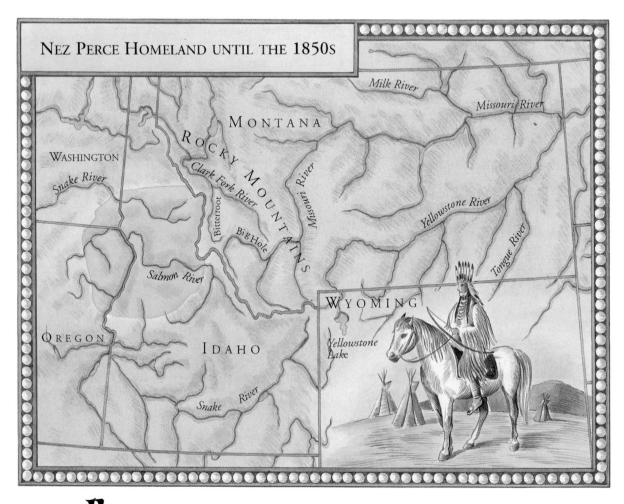

Bounded by the Cascades and the Rocky Mountains, the Nez Perce thrived in the Plateau region of western North America.

lava bed by rivers draining the tall, snowcapped mountains. The land and climate were ideal for the Nez Perce. The Bitterroot Range of the Rockies formed a barrier against enemies approaching from the east. The mountains could be surmounted through only a few narrow, dangerous passes. Sheltered by the mountains, the climate of the Plateau is also milder than the cold winters of the Great Plains or the mountain valleys of the Rockies. The Bitterroots serve to break the snowstorms sweeping down from the arctic north. Winds from the Pacific Ocean rise over the Cascades and release most of their moisture in sheets of rain in the high mountains before reaching the Plateau country. So, the winds that buffet the Plateau are warm and dry, with little rain or snow falling on the land. Falling from the moist Pacific winds, heavy snows lie in deep drifts in the mountains until the spring thaw fills the streams with rushing water. The water then flows down the streams during the dry summer months. The valleys also temper the winters, although the low ground can become very warm in the summer.

In a broad, sweeping curve, the eastern rim of the Plateau is marked by the Bitterroot Range of the Rocky Mountains. From Yellowstone National Park the mountains extend north and west across Idaho and into Oregon. To the north, another ridge stretches west from the Bitterroots across the panhandle of Idaho until it finally merges with the more gentle terrain of eastern Washington. Several rivers wind through Idaho, including the Snake and Salmon Rivers.

Rising from the slopes of the Continental Divide in northwestern Wyoming, the Snake River flows across southern Idaho, its bed in the bottom of a very deep ravine, its rocky banks rising high on either side. The river then curves north cutting through mountains into Hells Canyon, a narrow canyon that plunges a mile down. Through Hells Canyon, the water tumbles in wild rapids and whirlpools. At the lower end of the canyon, the Snake is joined by the turbulent waters of the Salmon River. Forty miles downstream, the Clearwater River empties into the Snake River, which continues west into Washington State.

The Salmon River rises in the mountains of central Idaho. Winding west through the mountains for more than a hundred miles, its turbulent waters have made it known as the "River of No Return." To the north of the Salmon River is the valley of the Clearwater River, flowing between the Bitterroot and the Clearwater Mountains. The mountains receive enough rain to support a dense forest of evergreens. Willow, cedar, and swamp alder grow lower in the valley. The Clearwater forms a great ravine with occasional rapids and canyons, as well as flat ground at the river bends, overgrown with scrub willow, wild rose, and other small trees and shrubs. Cottonwood, fir, and pines are also scattered along the river. Throughout the region are grassy hills and hollows, dotted with clumps of tall pines.

From early spring until midsummer, the country is splashed with colorful trees and wildflowers such as yellow sunflowers and purple shooting stars. There are blue bells, Indian paintbrush, and yellow lupine as well. Amid the profusion of flowers are several plants that the Nez Perce gathered for food, including the pink bitterroot and biscuitroot. Most important was the camas, which carpeted the meadows so thickly with blue flowers that they appeared to be small lakes.

The land also abounded in wildlife. Elk, deer, mountain sheep, and bears roamed the hills. Grouse flourished in the high country

The streams that threaded through their homeland were an important source of food for the Nez Perce.

while ducks and geese flocked to the rivers and streams. Herds of antelope wandered the grasslands of the Plateau. People also caught many kinds of fish, notably salmon in spawning runs. For countless generations the Nez Perce made their home in this territory, and many continue to live in the land of their ancestors.

2. Camps and Villages

Many Nez Perce adopted tipis as practical homes that could be easily assembled and taken down.

THE NEZ PERCE WERE GROUPED INTO UPPER AND LOWER DIVISIONS, BASED largely on differences in their dialects. Made up of a number of bands, the Nez Perce lived in villages along creeks and rivers. They also made seasonal migrations through the deep canyons to hunt, fish, and gather plant foods. Permanent villages were rarely established on the uplands. Around 1800, just before they came into significant contact with people of European descent, there were more than seventy villages with between thirty and two hundred people living in each. About three hundred additional town sites, including camps, have since been discovered.

Villages were made up of several extended families, including grandparents, aunts, uncles, and parents and their children. Each village was led by a chief, or headman, generally the oldest able-bodied male. He was assisted by several highly regarded younger men. Most often, chiefs inherited their positions, but occasionally a council replaced an inept leader with a more qualified man. Chiefs had to conduct themselves in an exemplary manner. They were held in high esteem if they were generous to others. Serving as the spokesmen of the village, they resolved conflicts and looked after the general welfare of the people. Families usually dispensed their own justice in dealing with crimes against them, but chiefs and councils sometimes exiled individuals who continued to commit serious offenses. Although they wielded considerable power, chiefs never opposed the wishes of their council, which included the heads of the families in the village. Shamans, or medicine men, were the leaders in some villages, but their authority was severely restricted by the councils that had elected them.

*W*ise and skilled older men who had distinguished themselves in battle usually served as leaders of Nez Perce bands.

The bands in a region often came together for hunting, fishing, and gathering, as well as for ceremonies. It was also essential that they unite to defend themselves against attack and to avenge a death. The bands allied under the leadership of a band council, made up of leaders and prominent warriors from each band. These councils chose leaders among themselves in the same manner as village councils. Sometimes, leadership was determined through heredity, but band councils also recognized courage, intelligence, and ability in selecting chiefs. Assisted by several proven warriors, the band leader was usually the chief of the largest village in the region. Composed of these loosely organized bands, the Nez Perce did not strongly unite as a tribe until after 1830 when they were forced to fight to save their homeland from settlers and soldiers.

Pit Houses and Other Dwellings

The Nez Perce of the early days constructed at least four different kinds of houses, including a communal longhouse, a lodge for menstruating women, a special house for unmarried men, and a cone-shaped tipi. They also put up temporary shelters as they migrated seasonally. During the summer months when they moved in search of food, the Nez Perce built lean-tos by covering poles with woven mats. On long hunting trips, they put up brush shelters as well. When they settled in villages for the winter, the Nez Perce placed a framework of long poles over pits and covered it with mats, bark, or grass. Called a pit house, the floor was dug beneath ground level— the floors of summer homes were slightly below grade and those of

Traditionally, the Nez Perce lived in pit houses. They were practical dwellings that stayed cool in the summer and warm in the winter.

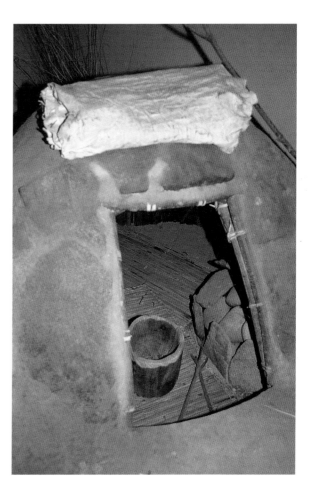

winter quarters were two to three feet in depth. Soil was piled around the sides of the dwelling to make a bermed wall for greater warmth.

Longhouses varied in size. They were generally about twenty to seventy feet in length and ten to fifteen feet wide. There were generally five or six of these houses in a village, each sheltering a number of families. Longhouses had a pair of ridgepoles running the length of the peak, with side poles laid at an angle, each a few inches apart,

*T*he Nez Perce also traditionally built longhouses, which were large enough to provide shelter for several families.

and lashed with ropes to form an A-frame. The narrow space between the ridgepoles served as a long, slender chimney for smoke rising from the cooking fires. Over this frame, people laid woven mats like shingles to shed the rain and snow. Sometimes, they covered the structure with a foot-thick layer of coarse grass instead of mats. They laid poles over this thick insulation to keep the wind from blowing off the mats or layers of grass. Finally, they laid dry grass and piled soil around the base of the longhouse. An entrance was left at one or both ends. During the winter, these were covered with skins.

Inside, a row of fires was kept burning in the center of the long-house, each about ten to twelve feet apart. Two families usually shared a fire. The Nez Perce used a fire starter that, according to folk stories, was given to them by Coyote. This tool consisted of a base with a shallow groove made from the root of the light-leaved willow or the stem of a tree known as "smoke wood." They used dried tips of red fir as twirling sticks and bits of brush or dry grass as tinder. By quickly turning the stick, they produced enough friction and heat to ignite the tinder. Although they could easily start a fire with this tool, they seldom let the lodge fires go out.

The interior was often left undivided, but occasionally families partitioned the longhouse into a double row of stall-like compart-ments, leaving a clear space down the middle. Near the walls they placed beds on mattresses of dry grass or the soft inner bark of cot-tonwood trees. Blankets were made from elk hides, which were tanned without removing the hair. Women spread mats on the floors and kept storage baskets at the head of their beds. They usually hung clothing from the rafters. For greater warmth during the winter, people often lined the inside walls of the house with skins.

Every village had one or more menstrual lodges. During the winter months, women stayed in these lodges when they had their periods and before and after childbirth. In the summer or when on the trail, women moved into a tipi set up some distance from the camp for this purpose. Men were not allowed near the menstrual lodge. While secluded in these lodges, women had to cook their own meals, and they were not permitted to touch anything used by others. About twenty feet in diameter, these circular lodges were made by laying poles over a hole about five to six feet deep. Covering the poles with grass and soil, a round opening served as a doorway. The floor was covered with mats, and beds were along the sides.

Through the winter, unmarried men, fourteen years of age or older, lived in special lodges. About ten to twelve feet in diameter and three feet deep, these lodges were covered with poles and grass with a sloped passage for a doorway. Inside, the floors were covered with a thick bed of grass, and heated stones were piled in the middle. In the morning, some of the men heated the stones in an outdoor fireplace. They then brought the stones inside and, while still hot, splashed them with water. Then anyone living there who wished could have a sweat bath before rising for the day. The Nez Perce always located these lodges near a stream so they could plunge into the cold water afterward. As many as fifteen young men stayed in each of these houses. Because of the close quarters, each person only needed a robe to keep warm through the night.

A view of a Nez Perce camp along the Yellowstone River in present-day Montana. This photograph was taken in 1871.

The Nez Perce also constructed small sweat houses along streams for use by both women and men. They bent supple willows to form a dome, which they then covered with grass and sod. Sometimes, an individual put up a small, temporary sweat house of willow branches covered with a blanket.

After they acquired horses, the Nez Perce began to travel and trade more widely and to build larger pit houses—some as long as 100 feet—during the winter. Lewis and Clark described one building that was 150 feet long. They also adopted tipis, especially when they went on hunting or fishing trips. Tipis were easier to set up, take down, and transport. While living along the rivers in pit houses, they

The natural world fulfilled all of the Nez Perce's housing needs. Tall trees, stripped of bark, served as ideal lodge poles.

fished, hunted, and gathered. With food plentiful and close at hand, they had little need to move very often. However, as they began to journey farther eastward onto the Great Plains to hunt buffalo, they chose to live in tipis which were better suited to a nomadic way of life. Made of wooden poles and covered with buffalo hides, a tipi could easily be transported as a travois (tra VOY). A travois consisted of two poles, the ends of which were strapped to the horse while the other ends dragged along the ground.

To make tipis, men cut long, straight, slender trees and stripped the bark to make lodge poles. After the poles had dried in the sun, they were dragged to the village. The women tied the ends of three poles together and raised them, spreading out the bottom ends. Once the supports were upright they placed eight to ten smaller poles in the gaps to make the cone-shaped frame. To make the covering, women spread fresh buffalo hides on the ground and scraped away the fat and flesh with bone or antler knives. After the skins had dried in the sun, they scraped off the shaggy brown hair. They soaked the stiff hides in water for a few days and then vigorously rubbed them with a mixture of animal fat, brains, and liver. After rinsing them in water, they repeatedly worked the hides to further soften them. Finally, they smoked the hides over a fire, which gave the skins a light tan color.

Several women laid out about fifteen tanned hides and carefully stitched them together to make the tipi's covering. Wrapped around the frame and held together with wooden pins, the covering had two wing-shaped flaps at the top that were opened to form a smoke hole. The flaps were closed to keep out the rain. The U-shaped doorway was also covered with a hide. The Nez Perce often placed the tipi in a pit about two feet deep, especially in the winter. They also hung a buffalo hide dew cloth on the inside walls from about shoulder height down to the ground. The dew cloth formed a pocket of insulating air. With a fire burning in the center of the earthen floor and buffalo robes lining the walls, tipis stayed warm throughout the coldest months.

Working together, several women could quickly erect or take down a tipi in minutes. They strapped one end of the poles to a horse's shoulders and allowed the other ends to drag behind it. They tied the folded cover and other belongings across the poles.

Children and old people were sometimes also carried on the travois as the Nez Perce moved from one camp to another. Household goods had to be light and durable. Pottery could be broken on their long journeys, so the Nez Perce began to store food, clothing, and other belongings in rawhide pouches called parfleches (par FLESH es). They carried water in animal skins and brought the soft lining of a buffalo stomach for cooking meat and vegetables.

Appaloosa Horses

Each year, Nez Perce bands made a hunting journey from the Plateau country to the Great Plains. With horses, they were now able to travel more easily. Hunters could also kill more buffalo, with less danger to themselves as they galloped after the herds. As a result the tribe had more food, and people enjoyed greater wealth. Although they con-

*T*o this day, the Nez Perce raise Appaloosa horses, which stand as important symbols of their independent way of life.

tinued to live in settled villages, the Nez Perce could also ride longer distances to raid the camps of their enemies and to trade with other tribes.

Horses brought a great deal of convenience to daily life. A few days each year, people rode horses to the meadows and used them to haul camas back to their homes. They also hunted deer and antelope on horseback and rode their favorite mounts to visit other villages. Horses would never have become so important to the Nez Perce if they did not live in excellent country for raising the animals. During the summers, the foothills offered fine grazing lands with abundant water, and during the mild winters, the valleys offered shelter and enough food for the horses to thrive all year on the open range. There were few predators, such as wolves and mountain lions, and the surrounding mountains acted as natural barriers that kept the horses from straying and enemy raiders from stealing them.

By intelligently managing their herds, primarily through careful breeding, the Nez Perce raised large numbers of horses renowned for their speed and endurance. They sold horses of poor quality and gelded, or castrated, stallions that were not suited for breeding. Through trade, they also brought in breeding stock from New Mexico, the state of Chihuahua, Mexico, and later California. Over time, they developed horses that were larger and better proportioned than the usual ponies of the Indians on the Great Plains. Native Americans favored bold markings, notably pintos and light-colored mounts. Over time, the Nez Perce favored a kind of distinctive spotted horse that came to be called the Appaloosa. It is believed that the name derives from the Palouse River in eastern Washington—the heart of the country where the beautiful horses were raised a century ago. The term may come from the French *pelouse*, meaning green meadows with abundant grass. However, it may also have derived from the Nez Perce *peluse* for "something sticking up out of the water" referring to a rock formation in the river. The Nez Perce continue to raise these exceptional horses in the Plateau country of Idaho.

3. Lifeways

Following the course of the
sun from dawn to dusk, Nez
Perce life centered around the
natural rhythms of the day.

Cycle of Life

Among the Nez Perce, each season came with its own set of tasks and rituals. In early spring, men trudged on snowshoes to hunt game and paddled canoes down the Snake and other rivers to catch salmon. As the days warmed, women dug roots in the valleys and the men caught fish closer to home. From midsummer through autumn, people hunted, fished, and gathered foods in the highlands. They occasionally ventured into the rolling hill country of Montana to pursue buffalo. Some bands remained on the plains for several years, but most returned to their villages where they settled in for the winter until the cycle began again in early spring. Similarly, families and bands continued the cycle of life. Women gave birth and raised their children, who in turn grew up and had children of their own. And from one generation to the next, old people told stories as the children gathered around the flickering yellow light of the fire.

Birth. When a woman was about to have a baby, female relatives instructed her in the best ways to protect her health and that of the newborn. These older women encouraged her to exercise vigorously, take baths in hot and cold water, and use medicinal herbs.

They also reminded her of the taboos. It was believed that the expectant mother should not touch or gaze upon deformed animals or people—or her baby might have a similar misfortune. She was also told not to tie knots or perform similar tasks that might symbolize difficulty in labor.

*T*o hunt buffalo on the Great Plains, the Nez Perce seasonally followed a well-worn trail winding along the river and through Lolo Pass.

The mother usually delivered her baby in a small house set apart from the rest of the village. A midwife or female relative assisted her, but if she had difficulty, a shaman came to her aid. This shaman had special powers and rituals for helping in the delivery.

After the baby was born, its umbilical cord was placed in a small hide container and attached to the cradleboard. The Nez Perce believed that it was bad luck to destroy such an important part of the infant's body. Relatives brought gifts and hosted feasts in honor of the mother and baby, especially if the child was her firstborn.

Shortly after birth, babies were placed on cradleboards where they remained most of the time until they were old enough to walk. Mothers could easily carry their babies on cradleboards. When they were working, they could prop the cradleboard against the pit house or hang it from a tree. Babies could then watch their mothers cook at the fire or gather roots in the meadow. Mothers nursed their babies for several years, gradually weaning them with softened meats and vegetables. When teething, babies chewed on tough gristle.

Childhood. Children were named after prominent ancestors in the hope that the name would influence their growth and maturity. Children often had nicknames as well. A naming ceremony with gift giving was held at the onset of puberty.

After babies were weaned, their grandparents usually cared for them, and they became very attached to each other. Children were generally very formal with their parents, but often joked with their grandparents. They were considered equals. In fact, the Nez Perce used the same term to refer to grandparents and grandchildren.

*T*raditionally, Nez Perce mothers placed their babies in ornately decorated cradleboards, which could easily be carried about the camp.

Children learned most of their life skills from their grandparents. Grandfathers usually taught the boys how to hunt, fish, and ride horses, as well as take part in sweat baths. Other relatives made sure the boys were properly instructed. Grandmothers taught the girls how to manage the household and to provide food and clothing for their families. Grandparents often told stories so young people might learn about the history and ways of the Nez Perce. Aunts, uncles, cousins, and older brothers and sisters also helped in teaching the children. In fact, children spent a great deal of time with their cousins, whom they considered brothers and sisters.

*F*rom an early age, boys were raised to become skilled hunters and warriors—with bows and arrows as well as clubs and shields.

Children were generally awakened before sunrise no matter what the season. Aunts and uncles made sure they took hot and cold baths to strengthen their bodies. Sometimes, relatives lightly switched and lectured children to ensure proper conduct.

Coming-of-Age. As they approached adolescence, young people were sent out to seek a vision from a guiding spirit. If they experienced a vision, they were assured of a good and prosperous life. However, if they did not have a vision, it was believed that they were destined for an undistinguished future. Youths often went out many times before they received a vision.

As she reached puberty, a girl underwent an elaborate ceremony. Isolated in a special house, she was attended by her mother and other female relatives. Friends and relatives were told that she was about to become a woman. During this time, she was encouraged to keep busy and to strive for positive thoughts. It was believed that whatever she did at this time would influence her future life. Her meals were cooked on a separate fire, and she went outside for only brief periods after dark. She could touch herself only with a scratcher, elaborately carved for this occasion. After a week or so, she was formally welcomed back into the community as a woman, now ready for marriage. Friends and family presented her with gifts and new clothes.

Marriage. Family heads often arranged marriages, with betrothals occasionally made during childhood. Wealth and social standing were considered important in matchmaking. When a young man became interested in a young woman, members of his family met and decided if she came from an acceptable family. If so, they reviewed each of their family histories to make sure they were not related in any way, because marriage was forbidden even among distant relatives. If another son or daughter had already married into the family, the proposed marriage was viewed more favorably, because additional marriages would strengthen the bond between the two families. Sometimes, two families were linked by marriages between several daughters and sons.

In some instances, an older female relative of the young man acted as a go-between with the young woman's family. If the family agreed to the marriage, the go-between moved in with them for a while to observe if the young woman was acceptable as a wife. During this time, the young man and woman visited each other, and their families sometimes gathered for feasts. If the couple and their families got along, they held a wedding ceremony and exchanged gifts.

Couples could reside with either set of parents, but most often they lived with the husband's family. Divorce was permitted but discouraged, especially as time went by and the families formed cooperative bonds.

Death. When a prominent man thought he was nearing death, he announced who would receive his wealth and guardian spirits, known as Wyakin. He might also suggest which sons should assume the positions he held in the tribe.

After a person died, the body was carried on a travois to a burial site on a slope overlooking the village which was usually located near a water source.

Upon a death, a crier announced the news and female relatives began to wail in grief. Friends and family gathered around the deceased and mourned until the body was washed, adorned with red face paint, dressed in new clothes, and buried the following day. Wrapped in a robe, the body was carried on a horse-drawn travois to a grave dug on a high slope overlooking the village. Cherished possessions were buried with the body, and occasionally a favorite horse was killed at the grave.

After burial, the family of the deceased hosted a feast and distributed his or her property. A man had probably owned horses, robes, necklaces, and weapons, while a woman would have had beaded bags, robes, and cooking utensils. Family members presented additional gifts to the mourners.

After the funeral feast, those who had prepared the body for burial ritually purified themselves. The spouses of the deceased cut their hair short and put on old clothing. They made a point not to laugh or even appear happy in public. They were not allowed to remarry for at least a year. To diminish the pain of their loss, the spouse and family did not mention the name of the deceased. Occasionally, the house was abandoned or destroyed, and new furnishings were acquired. At the end of the year of mourning, relatives formally presented the spouse with new clothes and sometimes a new mate, if one was available in their family. If not, the spouse was encouraged to marry someone else.

Warfare

War was a continual reality for the Nez Perce. Living in a region that abounded in food—wildlife and plants—they fought to protect their territory from their neighbors. While the Walla Walla, Yakima, and Cayuse were generally allies, the Nez Perce were always in conflict with the Shoshone who lived to the south. They occasionally battled the Flathead tribes to the north, although they enjoyed times

Often in conflict with the Shoshone and other neighboring tribes, bands of warriors galloped off to battle on horseback.

of peace and friendly exchange with them as well. Nez Perce war parties also occasionally swept into the northern Great Plains to fight the Blackfeet and the Crow. Having acquired horses before the eastern tribes, they also had to deal with raiders attempting to steal their valuable mounts. The Nez Perce were often joined by Flathead

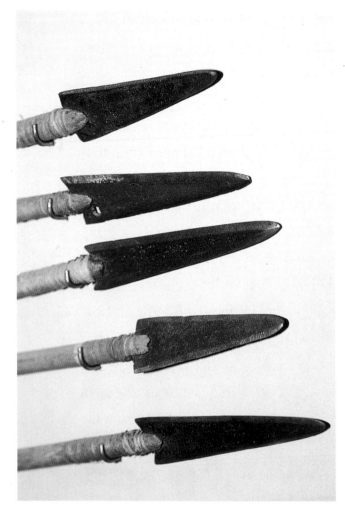

Men chipped stones—usually flint or obsidian—which sharpened easily into points. They were then attached to arrows with sinew.

tribes, especially the Spokane and Coeur d'Alene, in annual journeys into buffalo country. The trips usually began in the spring and returned the following year along three trails through Coeur d'Alene territory and across the Bitterroot Mountains. Women and children often accompanied the men. Occasionally there were fierce battles with the Plains tribes during these journeys.

Warriors relied on bows and arrows. Men made three kinds of bows, two of which were backed with sinew from a deer or other animal for greater strength. They fashioned the most remarkable bows from the horn of a mountain sheep. First, they split the horn and removed a coiled strip of material, which they steamed, stretched, and straightened into the proper, curved shape. Then they glued on deer sinew. The glue was made by boiling scrapings from the skin of steelhead trout or occasionally blood from the backbone of a sturgeon. They twisted deer sinew to make the bowstring.

For arrow shafts, they used serviceberry branches, which they heated and straightened, and then polished with tufa, a soft, porous rock found near streams and springs. They chipped arrowheads from flint and obsidian, and attached them to the shaft with sinews. They fitted each arrow with three eagle or hawk feathers, which were also tied on with sinew. They often painted decorative bands on the shaft near the feathers. They carried their arrows in a quiver made from the skin of an otter, coyote, or cougar. Originally, the Nez Perce used a single quiver, but they adopted the double quiver used by the Crow, with separate compartments for the bow and arrows. When shooting, they usually held the bow and two or three arrows in the left hand. Sometimes, warriors poisoned the arrowheads with rattlesnake venom.

Warriors also armed themselves with spears about eight feet long and fitted with a stone or bone point. They also wielded clubs with stone heads. One type of battle club had a point on each end and a groove in the middle for tying the club to a handle with rawhide.

Another type of club, made from a fist-sized boulder wrapped in an animal skin and attached to an eighteen-inch handle, was used for both warfare and hunting.

For armor, warriors relied on shields, helmets, and a kind of battle tunic. About fourteen inches in diameter, a shield was made by stretching a fresh elk hide over a hoop. When the skin dried, it fitted tightly over the circular frame. Men decorated their shields with paintings, scalps, and feathers. From the tough hides of elk, they also made helmets that draped down in back to protect the neck as well as the head. In early times, the Nez Perce warriors wore a sleeveless, knee-length elk-hide tunic. After the introduction of horses, however, they usually wore only a breechcloth and war bonnet made from the head of a wolf or buffalo adorned with eagle feathers, bear claws, and other decorations. Sometimes, they wore a wreath or streamers of eagle feathers.

As they prepared for war, men stripped to their breechcloths and painted their faces and bodies in bright colors. They painted a line of red along the part in their hair and across their foreheads. Men rubbed a mixture of white clay and saliva into their hair and painted their faces and bodies, usually in various orange and red patterns. Around their necks, they hung a war knife and a bone whistle that was blown only in battle. Warriors also wore feathers and fur, as well as animal teeth and claws, to strengthen their bond with their guardian spirits. They favored white mounts, or Appaloosas if these were not available, as warhorses. They painted their horses with streaks of red, blue, black, and yellow, and adorned their heads and tails with streamers of feathers.

Hunting, Fishing, and Gathering

When the days began to warm in the spring, salmon began to run, or swim upriver, to lay their eggs. Although they continued to hunt, the Nez Perce concentrated on fishing during this time of year. Men did most of the fishing, using a hook and line. They also speared and netted fish from canoes and dipping platforms on major streams. Men caught salmon in brush traps and weirs, which were large enclosures constructed by the village across a stream. One person regulated the fishing and divided the catch. Women helped to split, sun dry, smoke, and store the salmon. The Nez Perce caught many kinds of salmon, including chinook, coho, chum, and sockeye, and many types of trout, notably cutthroat, lake, and steelhead. They also caught suckers, whitefish, sturgeons, squawfish, and lamprey.

With bows and arrows, men hunted elk, deer, and moose. They also stalked mountain goats and sheep, as well as black bears and grizzlies. Hunting was often difficult on the hot and dry Plateau. To get near the animals in the open valleys, they often disguised themselves in animal skins. Or a group surrounded a herd of elk or deer, gradually tightening the circle, until the animals were trapped and more easily taken. Smaller animals, including rabbits, squirrels, badgers, and marmots, were also hunted. Birds such as ducks, geese, sage hens, and grouse were hunted for their meat, and birds of prey

*E*xperienced hunters tried their luck in the forests, which, unlike the dry and open plains, abounded in game.

were prized for their feathers which had ceremonial uses. Occasionally, men trapped large animals in deadfalls and smaller animals in snares. When they became skilled horsemen, the Nez Perce sent a yearly party to the Great Plains to hunt buffalo.

The rugged terrain—steep canyons and cliffs, as well as dry valleys—added to the difficulty of gathering plants in the Plateau region. In the summer, women used sticks to dig biscuitroots, or couse, on grassy hillsides. They ground and boiled the roots into soups or made the powdered roots into cakes to be eaten later. Through the warm months, they also gathered wild onions, carrots, and bitterroots. Women harvested many kinds of berries, including huckleberries, serviceberries, and currants. Pine nuts, sunflower seeds, and black moss were also important foods. Toward the end of summer, the bands came together to gather camas lily bulbs, their most important root crop. They steamed the lily bulbs and made them into a sweet dough or mush.

By November, people had settled into their villages for the winter. Now they would live off the supplies of food they had put aside in baskets or parfleche bags. The baskets and bags were safely stored in cache pits dug into hillsides and lined with bark or grass.

To prepare meals, women baked meat and roots in large earthen ovens. Or they boiled food in baskets filled with water in which they placed heated stones. They also broiled meat and fish over the fire on wooden frames or sticks. They often crushed roots in a mortar with pestles made from stones or wood, and made the pulp into loaves or biscuits that stored well. The loaves were later cooked in soups and stews.

Elk Stew

The Nez Perce made soups, stews, and a variety of other dishes. Besides salmon and other fish, the Nez Perce ate various meats such as elk and buffalo. This recipe is similar to a traditional meal and is still prepared by women for their families.

Ingredients

3 lbs. of elk (or beef stew meat), cubed

3 tbl. bacon grease or cooking oil

2 medium onions, chopped

2 cloves of garlic, chopped

1/2 tsp. oregano

1 tsp. salt

1/4 tsp. pepper

1 quart water

6 carrots, sliced

1/2 lb. mushrooms, sliced

5 potatoes, cubed

1 1/2 cups celery, chopped

Directions

Brown elk meat in bacon grease or cooking oil in a large pan. Remove. Saute onions and garlic in grease or oil until translucent. Simmer meat, onions, garlic, along with oregano, salt, pepper, and about one quart of water for 2 1/2 hours, or until meat is tender. Add vegetables and cook until done. Serves about six people.

Women stored food, such as dried buffalo meat, in leather pouches called parfleches, which could easily be carried from one camp to another.

Clothing and Jewelry

The Nez Perce wore clothing made from deer, elk, and buffalo skins. Like the Plains Indians, men wore moccasins and breech-cloths. When the weather turned cold, they also put on long-sleeved shirts and leggings. The leather clothing was fringed along the seams and decorated with porcupine quills, beads, and paint. For warmth men wrapped themselves in buffalo robes tanned with the fur still on the skin. The robes were also used as lounging mats and saddle blankets. Men wore jewelry, such as necklaces of bear claws, wolf teeth, and deer hooves, and arm and leg bands.

Women wore loosely fitting buckskin dresses and moccasins that were not as lavishly decorated as men's clothing. Dresses had cap sleeves and hung from the shoulders to the ankles. The hem and side seams were fringed. Women adorned their dresses with bands of beadwork and attached elk teeth, small pieces of copper, and other ornaments. Women occasionally wore leggings. As they traveled widely on horseback, the Nez Perce began to wear more finely tailored skin garments adorned with beads, shells, elk teeth, and other decorative touches. Women also wore large basketry hats made from dried leaves and grasses, into which they wove designs. They attached deerskin ribbons to the crown and tied pendants and tassels to the ribbons. Although women wore less jewelry than men, they did hang shell discs from their ears.

Both men and women parted their long hair in the middle and made two braids on either side of their heads. Men's hair was cut in

*T*he Nez Perce still adorn their clothing, such as this pair of leather gloves, with fringes and decorative beadwork.

Among the adornments on this buckskin dress are intricate rows of dyed porcupine quills.

bangs across the forehead, but the women did not have bangs. Men often had strips of otter or ermine fur, shells, and other ornaments woven into their braids. Men also carefully pulled out any facial hair.

Women and men often painted their faces and bodies, especially in red and orange, simply to enhance their appearance. However, sometimes, the paintings related to the animal that was their guardian spirit. They painted their eyelids, foreheads, and the part in their hair a brilliant red. Occasionally, women made designs of lines and dots on their skin.

Handicrafts

The Nez Perce made many useful tools, baskets, and household utensils. They fashioned a digging stick for unearthing roots. About two and a half feet long, this stick had a curved, fire-hardened point and a bone, horn, or stone handle.

Women were especially skilled weavers. They wove baskets used for pounding roots with a wooden tool called a mortar. They ate food out of baskets or wooden bowls with spoons and ladles made of the horns of mountain sheep or buffalo. They made floor mats and house coverings from the long, slender leaves of cattails or tule. For light flexible baskets, they often used Indian hemp or beargrass. In recent years, they have begun to use corn husks. They fashioned carrying baskets, which were flat like wallets, and cylinder-shaped pack baskets. They also made winnowing baskets and watertight cooking baskets, along with cups and food bowls. They wove distinctive fez-shaped hats, which reflect their finest work.

Nez Perce women also wove and wore basketry hats made from dried leaves and grasses.

The long tradition of Nez Perce handicrafts thrives to this day, as is evident in this patterned purse.

The Nez Perce made many tools and weapons of bone and horn. Elk horn wedges, pounded with wooden mallets, were used to split wood, chop down trees, and hollow out canoes. After boiling bones to remove the fat, they made them into awls for punching holes in leather, braiding ropes, and weaving baskets. They fashioned the long bones of the sandhill crane into whistles and used the bones of other birds for tools as well. They fitted sharp bones onto fishing spears and used bone tools for flaking arrowheads. They also made dice and gaming pieces from bones.

Along with flaking, or chipping, sharp arrowheads and knives from stone, men hollowed out river boulders to make pestles, most often shaped like bowls or boats. Used for pounding roots, pestles required so much work to make that they were passed down through generations of families. The Nez Perce occasionally made stone mortars, but more often they used wood.

They carved pipes from soft stones—either soapstone which had a bluish or yellowish cast, or tufa which had a spongy texture. They often made wooden stems which fitted into a small hole in the pipe bowl. Smoking was a sacred part of their ceremonies. A stone pipe with a stem about three feet long was solemnly handed from one person to another during peace talks.

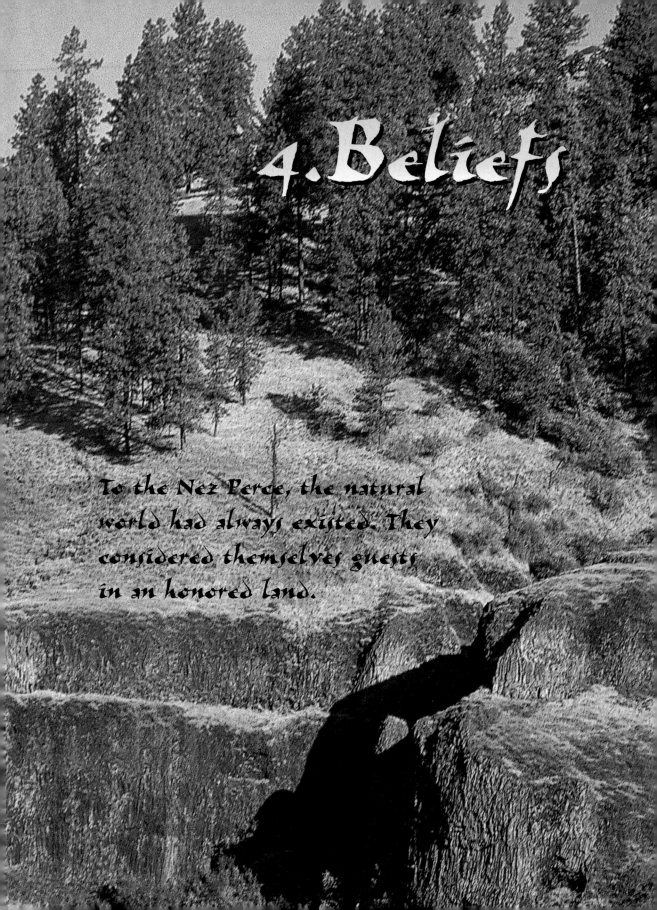

4. Beliefs

To the Nez Perce, the natural
world had always existed. They
considered themselves guests
in an honored land.

THE NEZ PERCE BELIEVED THAT THE MOUNTAINS, VALLEYS, AND RIVERS HAD always existed, and that all the plants, creatures, and natural elements such as stones, water, and the landscape itself were closely related. They had a deep spiritual relationship with the earth. Spirits could be good or evil and lived everywhere—in trees, hills, and streams. Those dwelling in trees and streams tended to be good. Some trees became shrines visited by shamans.

The sun was honored as a guardian spirit and a great source of wisdom, especially for shamans, who sought its good will. The sun is believed to have told one shaman, "Your knowledge will be exactly like my light." Most individuals in the tribe also had a guardian spirit, known as a Wyakin, who kept them from harm and often provided help. Warriors prayed to the Wyakin before going into battle, and women prayed for good fortune when gathering food. People often carried medicine bundles, which were small pouches with objects that symbolized their Wyakin. When young men and women came of age, they left the village in search of their own Wyakin through a spirit vision. They found a place where they could be alone, without food or water. They waited for their Wyakin to reveal itself through a dream or a natural event such as a flash of lightning. When they returned to the village, they did not speak of their Wyakin. But throughout their lives, they followed special rules and prayed to their Wyakin in times of need.

The Nez Perce also told stories of monsters, giants, and dwarfs. Hunters brought back tales of cannibal giants from their trips to the Great Plains. Coyote, the mystical hero of the Nez Perce, is believed

*T*he rushing rivers, the far-reaching trees—to the Nez Perce these were the dwelling places of powerful spirits.

to have destroyed these creatures. It was also believed that a handful of little men, no more than two feet tall, lived in the mountains. Sometimes they helped people in need. At other times, they stirred up mischief and made travelers lose their way.

$\mathbf{A}$mong the Nez Perce, women could also be shamans, esteemed figures who possessed spiritual powers to heal and bring about good fortune.

People believed in a number of superstitions, such as setting fire to trees to bring good weather. They also thought that the cooing of doves forecast the running of the salmon. Before a hunt, they took sweat baths or hung deer antlers from trees to bring good luck. They picked up stones with unusual shapes or colors and carried them as good luck charms. The Nez Perce also had great faith in dreams, which they considered a means of communication from the spiritual world. These were not everyday dreams, but brilliant visions induced by patient vigils, fasting, and ecstatic celebration.

Whether male or female, shamans were endowed with great spiritual powers. It was believed that they could change the weather, bring misfortune upon people, and cure the sick and injured through songs and herbal medicines. Shamans acquired their positions through heredity or from guardian spirits. Generally, an old shaman chose a young relative, a boy or girl, as the successor to whom he would teach the songs and secrets of his powers. Along with the song he had received at his own sacred vigil many years ago, he had inherited songs and received some in dreams.

Most often, shamans treated patients with a sweat bath followed by a plunge in the cold waters of a nearby stream. Or they prescribed a warm bath, especially for skin conditions. For rheumatism and afflictions of the limbs, they packed the arm or leg in grass and soil, and warmed it over a roasting pit. They set broken bones with poles tied together and covered with deerskin. Shamans also used a variety of herbal remedies to effectively relieve fevers, diarrhea, and common illnesses. They capably applied poultices of pounded roots to cuts and sprains, and stopped bleeding with a spider web dressing.

Rites and Ceremonies

The Nez Perce often held dances and other ceremonies when they happened to meet a friendly tribe, such as the Yakima, Walla Walla, or Umatilla. There was also a regular cycle of dancing among the tribes living in the territory. Certain spots were traditionally regarded as dancing places—usually open, level ground near the mouth of a stream. Sometimes, ceremonies were held under a large tent, resembling a longhouse, perhaps fifteen feet wide, with the sides partly open. Women and children sat in front and men stood behind them to watch the ceremonies. Along with singing and dancing to the beating of drums, these celebrations were also an occasion for councils, horse racing, and gambling, as well as hunting and gathering.

The Nez Perce often expressed their deeply held beliefs at religious ceremonies, such as this gathering with a shaman named Two Moons.

Every winter, the Nez Perce held the Waiyatsit, a supernatural-power dance and the most significant religious event of the year. In this ritual, men and women represented their Wyakin through dance and sound. They painted themselves and dressed like the animal that embodied their Wyakin. If the dancer was portraying Coyote, he might paint his hair white and his forehead red with red streaks extending back. By carefully observing any dancers who had recently acquired a Wyakin, others in the group could guess the identity of their spirits. Contests were often held to determine who had received the greatest powers from their Wyakin.

The Nez Perce also held the Páhamn, or War Dance, in which only men participated. This dance was also often held on the camas meadows of the Weippe Prairie near present-day Moscow, Idaho, when buffalo hunters departed for the plains. In this ancient war dance there were two lines of dancers. A leader danced to a rhythm kept by rubbing a stick against a notched rod. The Nez Perce later adopted the dance and songs of the Crow Indians after Nez Perce warriors crept up to their camp during the night and secretly observed their ritual. Each participant sang his individual song based on his guardian spirit. As in ancient times, a farewell song was sung before the lodge of each warrior in the war party.

Held about four times a year, the Scalp Dance was the most significant intertribal ceremony. Everyone celebrated when victorious warriors returned with captives, scalps, and other trophies, whether they were renowned chiefs leading hundreds of warriors or a young man and his small band. Scalps of the Blackfeet and Shoshone, who

*W*hen a war party returned to camp, the Nez Perce often held a Scalp Dance in which they celebrated victory over their enemies.

had long been enemies of the Nez Perce, were especially prized. Scalps of the Salish were also valued during the occasional wars with them. Most songs referred to the scalps taken in the conflict and the female captives who were to become wives of the victors. Lasting five or six days, the celebration included feasts, gambling, and horse races. With scalps and other trophies raised on a pole, the dance began in the afternoon and continued until sunset. Forced to dance and sing with everyone else, the captives were also tortured, but afterward their wounds were dressed. Never killed, at the conclusion of the Scalp Dance prisoners became the property of their captors and were generally well treated thereafter.

Games

The Nez Perce enjoyed many different games. The hand game known as *lóhmit* was a favorite among the men. Seated in two rows facing each other, the men each beat a log placed between them to keep time to a song. Each side had ten counting sticks. There were also two sets of small pieces made from the leg bones of a deer. Each set consisted of two bones—one plain and the other decorated with a black ring of deerskin. The leader handed out the sets to two players, who shuffled the pieces and then held out their closed hands. The object was to guess which hand held which piece. When both sets of bones had been correctly guessed the sides changed. Counting sticks were handed over for losses. The side that first gave up all its sticks lost the game.

Women especially liked to play dice. They used four dice—two marked with circles, known as *há-ma*, or men, and two with zigzag lines called *a-yat*, or women. Before the game, they decided how many points would win the contest. Two or more players sat opposite each other on a blanket, and each player threw the dice in turn. They scored two points when the same four designs turned up and one point when a pair of designs turned up.

*S*torytelling was central to Nez Perce life. It helped explain the world around them and their living connection to the land.

The Nez Perce also played a hoop-and-pole game in which spears were thrown at a hoop as it rolled over smoothed ground. They also enjoyed a game similar to field hockey, played with curved bats and a leather ball stuffed with deer hair. Men and women competed against each other on level ground with goals made of piles of stones placed about fifteen feet apart at each end. Men from neighboring villages also played a game in which they lined up facing each other. With fifty to a hundred men on each side, they made fun of each other and then rushed together. Using only their feet and shoulders, but not their hands, they kicked and bumped each other. The line which gave way first lost the game.

Children liked to slide down snowy hills or grassy slopes on deerskins. They also spun tops made of a disc of bark through which a wooden peg was fitted. They played cat's cradle and other games with string. The elders often joined in the round of cat's cradle to amuse the children, and each string figure included a story.

Families always enjoyed coming together to listen to stories, especially during the long winters. Many of these stories recount the origin of the earth and the relationships among its creatures. Here is a story about how Coyote freed the salmon from the Swallow Sisters.

The Salmon and the Five Swallow Sisters

One hot summer, Coyote was resting in the shade of a tree. Gazing over the country, he told himself that he should take a swim in the chill waters of a river in a deep canyon. Making his way along a winding trail to the river, he plunged into the water and swam downstream through rapids and pools.

"This is so refreshing," Coyote told himself. "I think I'll keep swimming for a while."

However, he soon came to a stone dam built by the five Swallow Sisters who lived along the stream. Fierce, powerful, and jealous, the sisters would not allow anyone to pass by their home—even the salmon who swam upriver to lay their eggs. Thousands upon thousands of salmon came up from the ocean. Desperately, they flung themselves into the air. But no matter how hard they tried, they could not jump over the stone dam. Unable to swim upstream, the silvery fish gathered in the pools of calm water below the dam.

*S*almon spawned in the streams of the Plateau region, providing the Nez Perce with a reliable food source.

"It is not fair to keep the salmon from moving up the river," Coyote told himself. "They must be able to lay their eggs and have young salmon to provide food for the generations of people."

Yet Coyote knew that the sisters carefully guarded the dam, and they would peck out his eyes if he tried to break it down. So, he thought of a way to trick them. He swam to the bank, where he made a little raft of willow branches. With his great magic, he turned himself into a baby with black hair and bright eyes and dressed in white buckskin.

Drifting into the stream on the raft, he cried out, "Ah-ee, ah-ee. I am frightened and alone. My parents have gone to the buffalo lands and lost me."

At work in their house, the Swallow Sisters rushed down to the river.

"I want him! I want him!" they all cried when they saw the darling boy. But the eldest sister was the first to touch the raft, and she claimed him.

"We can all take care of him," suggested the second sister. Picking up the youngster, they eagerly carried him to the house.

Coyote thought to himself, "I am so clever. Living here with the Swallow Sisters, I will surely have a chance to tear down the dam."

However, the eldest sister said, "I am so happy to have a little son. We must be careful and never let him out of our sight."

They made a bed of soft grass for the child and sang to him all day. Clicking and clucking, they dangled bright feathers before his eyes and fed him fresh berries and roots.

Coyote became very annoyed with all this love and attention. He could hardly escape their loving embraces, let alone get near the dam. However, one day while lying in his crib, he noticed that all five Swallow Sisters were busy digging camas roots on the riverbank.

"I want a drink of water," he cried. "I want a drink of water."

"Son, we are very busy," the eldest sister called to him. "You are old enough to crawl to the river and get a drink for yourself."

He crawled on his hands and knees out of the lodge. As soon as he was out of sight, he changed back into Coyote and began smashing the dam with a large rock. Water rushed through the break, widening the hole, and the salmon eagerly slipped through the gap and swam upstream.

Hearing the hammering sounds of his stone and the rejoicing of the salmon, the Swallow Sisters swooped down to attack Coyote.

"Kill him!" the four younger sisters cried.

"But he is wearing the clothes of my baby," the eldest protested.

Indeed, Coyote had worked his magic so quickly that he still wore the white buckskin clothes. Confused and afraid, the Swallow Sisters backed away. They never rebuilt the dam and soon moved away.

Coyote called to the salmon, "I've broken the dam for your people. Now you must do me a favor. Come back and let me eat some of you."

But the salmon did not even thank him as they hurried up the river. Coyote was never rewarded for his good deed. But the river still flows clear and cold, and the salmon make their way upstream, year after year, providing abundant food for the generations of people who came to live there.

5. Changing World

The Nez Perce greatly relied on their horses. By 1877, however, freedom and mobility came to an end as they were forced to settle on reservations.

"No mountains, no springs, no clear running rivers. Thoughts come of the Wallowa where I grew up, of my own country when only the Indians were there, of tipis along the bending river, of the blue water lake, wide meadows with horse and cattle herds. From the mountain forests, voices seemed calling. I felt as dreaming. Not my living self."

—Yellow Wolf

William Clark of the Lewis and Clark expedition was the first person of European descent to visit the Nez Perce. The explorer was very impressed by the honesty and hospitality of their hosts. Having acquired horses from native peoples living to the south, the Nez Perce had already traded for European goods from other tribes. Not long after the encounter with the Lewis and Clark expedition in 1805, fur traders built posts at Walla Walla and Coeur d'Alene Lake. In 1836, Henry Spalding established a mission at the mouth of Lapwai Creek in the heart of Nez Perce territory. Soon, pioneers swarmed into the forests and prairies, gradually forcing the Nez Perce from their ancestral lands and changing their way of life.

After the Nez Perce helped Lewis and Clark in 1805, they established friendly relations with both French-Canadian and American fur traders, as well as missionaries and settlers who came into their territory. Over the next fifty years they became loyal allies of the United States, even as settlers poured into their territory. At the Walla Walla Council of 1855, they signed a treaty in which they gave away a portion of their ancestral country in exchange for money and an assurance that they could keep the rest of their sprawling lands—thirteen million acres. However, after signing treaties with several other Plateau tribes, Isaac Stevens, governor of the Washington Territory, immediately wrote a letter to an eastern newspaper declaring that the land was open for settlement. As settlers flooded into the region, Native Americans responded violently in the Plateau Indian War which raged from 1855 to 1858. However, most of the Nez Perce remained neutral. But this was not to last long. In 1861, gold was discovered in the land of the Nez Perce, and prospectors rushed into the region, ignoring the treaty of 1855. Both the settlers and the miners urged the U.S. government to allow them to claim more of the land.

In 1863, after failing to reach a new agreement, Governor Stevens managed to get a few signatures of tribal members on a document that came to be known as the Thief Treaty. In this fraudulent document, it was claimed that the Nez Perce had agreed to give up another seven million acres, including their land in the Wallowa Valley. Old Chief Joseph, a peaceful leader of the Wallowa band who had earlier converted to Christianity, was so angry that he tore up his Bible. Yet Old Chief Joseph and the other Nez Perce remained peaceful. In 1871, when Old Chief Joseph died, his son Joseph, who became widely known as Chief Joseph, became principal chief, concerned mainly with civic responsibilities, and his brother Ollikut became war chief. Both attempted to maintain their father's practice of nonviolent resistance, but the wave of settlers swarming onto Nez Perce land made this impossible. In 1875, the U.S. government

Chief Joseph, the proud Nez Perce leader who fought a losing war to save his homeland, posed for this photograph in 1903.

opened the territory for homesteaders and in May 1877, General Oliver Howard demanded that the Nez Perce relocate to a reservation within thirty days. Chief Joseph later stated, "It makes my heart sick when I remember all the good words that are broken promises."

Fearing a major war in which many Nez Perce would be killed, Chief Joseph urged his followers to comply with the ultimatum. He said, "I would give up everything rather than have the blood of my people on my hands." However, four settlers were killed in an act of vengeance. Other Nez Perce warriors then slaughtered fifteen more settlers. Chief Joseph reluctantly agreed to support the hostile warriors, as long as they promised not to kill women, children, or wounded men, or to take scalps. General Howard sent a group of cavalry under the command of Captain David Perry after the Nez Perce. Ignoring the Indians' truce flag, the soldiers fired, leading to the Battle of White Bird Canyon in 1877.

General Howard then led a larger force which pursued the warriors, including women and children, for nearly a month. The Nez Perce skillfully eluded capture by the soldiers along the rough banks of the Salmon River. The warriors killed every soldier in a scouting party lead by Lieutenant S. M. Rains. After an attack by soldiers, a band led by Looking Glass escaped the reservation and joined Chief Joseph's group on July 1. They outfought Howard and his troops in the Battle of Clearwater on July 11 and 12. Chief Joseph wished to return to the Wallowa Valley to defend his homeland, but in a council most warriors decided to make their way through the Bitterroot Mountains to join the Crow.

Pursued by more than 1,900 soldiers, the Nez Perce with fewer than 150 warriors and about 500 women and children fought their way into Montana. Under the leadership of Toohoolhoolzote, White Bird, and Poker Joe, they artfully evaded a barrier constructed by volunteers from Fort Missoula. The barricade became known as "Fort Fizzle."

The next major engagement came at the Battle of Big Hole, where White Bird shouted, "Fight! Shoot them down! We can shoot as well as any of these soldiers!" However, between sixty to ninety Nez Perce were killed before the bands were able to get away. A daring counterattack led by White Bird allowed the Nez Perce to escape. The great leader Yellow Wolf later described the attack, "The air was heavy with sorrow. Some soldiers acted with crazy minds."

After this engagement, Poker Joe replaced Looking Glass as the leading war chief and the Nez Perce traveled southeast, back into Idaho. On August 20, Ollikut led a raid on Howard's camp at Camas Creek, stampeding 200 pack mules to slow down their pursuers as they recovered the animals. In another council, the Nez Perce decided to travel north into Canada to seek refuge with Sitting Bull and his band of Sioux. They cut eastward through Targhee Pass into what is now Yellowstone National Park, then through the Absaroka Mountains.

Leading 350 cavalrymen from Fort Keogh, Montana, Colonel Samuel Sturgis engaged the Nez Perce in the Battle of Canyon Creek on September 13. But the warriors managed to fight off the attackers while the women and children escaped. Then the warriors slipped

*O*ld Fort Walla Walla was one of the frontier forts from which attacks against the Nez Perce and other tribes were organized and launched.

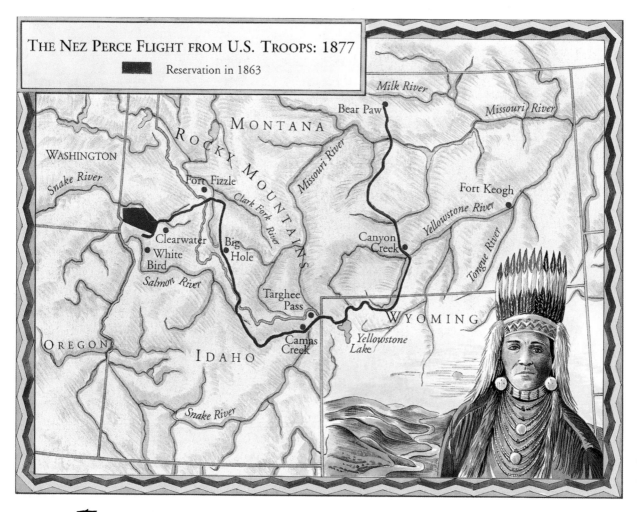

Reservation in 1863

Milk River

Missouri River

Bear Paw

MONTANA

ROCKY MOUNTAINS

WASHINGTON

Snake River

Fort Fizzle

Missouri River

Clark Fork River

Fort Keogh

Yellowstone River

Clearwater
White
Bird

Big
Hole

Canyon
Creek

Tongue River

Salmon River

Targhee
Pass

OREGON

IDAHO

Camas
Creek

Yellowstone
Lake

WYOMING

Snake River

For more than five months, Chief Joseph and the Nez Perce resisted capture in their desperate flight from U.S. soldiers.

away. As they continued northward, the Nez Perce fought other skirmishes with the soldiers. They also obtained badly needed provisions by raiding an army depot at Cow Island on the Missouri River. Just thirty miles from the Canadian border, they camped along the Snake River in the Bear Paw Mountains. On September 30, about 600 troops from Fort Keogh led by Colonel Nelson Miles finally caught up with the Nez Perce and attacked their camp. Both sides suffered tremendous losses. Chief Joseph and White Bird were the only chiefs to survive the onslaught which ended with the surrender of the Nez Perce on October 5, 1877.

In what became a famous speech, Chief Joseph declared, "I am tired of fighting. Our chiefs are killed. . . . The old men are all dead. It is the young men who say yes or no. He who led on the young men is dead. It is cold and we have no blankets. The little children are freezing to death. My people, some of them, have run away to the hills, and have no blankets, no food, no one knows where they are—perhaps freezing to death. I want to have time to look for my children and see how many of them I can find. Maybe I shall find them among the dead. Hear me, my Chiefs! I am tired, my heart is sick and sad. From where the sun now stands I will fight no more forever."

The Wallowa band was exiled to reservations in Oklahoma and Kansas and finally to the Colville Reservation in Washington. The rest of the tribe was sent to the reservation near Lapwai, Idaho. In 1800, there were about 6,000 people, but over the next hundred years, the Nez Perce were further devastated by disease, and only about 1,500

Nez Perce were alive in the early 1900s. The population has since recovered and there are now about 4,000 people, most of whom live on the Nez Perce Reservation near Lapwai, Idaho, or on the Colville Reservation.

Yet many people remembered the horrors of warfare. For years they mourned the loss of their loved ones. As a woman named Watatonmi recalled, "It was lonesome, the leaving. Husband dead, friends buried or held prisoners. I felt that I was leaving all that I had but I did not cry. You know how you feel when you lose kindred and friends through sickness—death. You do not care if you die. With us it was worse. Strong men, well women, and little children killed and buried. They had not done wrong to be so killed. We had asked to be left in our own homes, the homes of our ancestors. Our going with heavy hearts, broken spirits. But we would be free. . . . All lost, we walked silently on into the wintry night."

Nez Perce Language

The Nez Perce language belongs to the Sahaptian language family of the Columbia River region. Nez Perce is closely related to the languages of the Walla Walla, Yakima, and other tribes of the Plateau region. Today, the language is rarely spoken by younger members of the tribe.

The following examples are based primarily on the *Nez Perce Dictionary* by Haruo Aoki. Nez Perce is a complex and subtle language, but the following key, with some examples, will be a helpful guide to its pronunciation.

a	as in f*a*ther
e	as in p*a*n
i	as in t*i*n
o	as in g*o*
u	as in p*u*t
-	indicates that the preceding vowel is long. For example, *I-* is pronounced as in shine, not sister.

The consonants are generally pronounced as in English with the following exceptions:

c	as the *ts* in ha*ts*
l	voiceless *l*, like *sh* plus *l*
s̲	as in a*sh*
x̲	similar to *box*, but with a slight *ah* sound from the back of the throat
?	glottal stop, a catch in the throat, as in the slight pause between *uh oh*!
	Some glottalized consonants are also indicated by a '
´	stress mark to emphasize a vowel

The following are everyday words used by the Nez Perce.

arrow	cé-p
bird	payó-payó-
boy	há-cwal
buffalo, bison	qoq'á-lx̱
deer	?ímes
dog	ciqá'-mqal
doll	?ista?í-sta
eagle, bald	saq'antá-yx̱
elk	wisé-w
fire	?á-la
fish (salmon)	lé-wliks
food	hípt
forest (timber)	lé-qew
frog	wex̱wéqt
girl	pití-n
horse	sík'em
house	cóqoy
land	wé-tes
man	há-ma
moon	cik'etpememyé-ye hí-semtuks
mountain	mé-x̱sem
people	titó-qan
prairie	tex̱pé?m
quill, porcupine	sácas
river	pí-kun

sagebrush	qémqem
sky	ʔipelí-kt
snow	mé-qeʔ
star	x̱ic-íyu
sun	halx̱pamayá
turtle	ʔá-cix
water	kú-s
wind	há-tya
woman	ʔá-yat

Body Parts

arm, lower	káptkapt
arm, upper	kéhen
belly	ʔilú-t
chest	híni
ear	macáyo
elbow	kassáyno
eye	sílu
finger (hand)	ʔípsus
foot	ʔéx̱we
hair	sétey
head	hú-sus
knee	ʔí-mn
leg	wé-yux
mouth	hím
nose	nú-snu
shoulder	húhuy

6. New Ways

For this young girl, a bicycle is a great way to get around the reservation.

"Good words will not get my people a home where they can live in peace and take care of themselves."—Chief Joseph

For nearly 125 years, the Nez Perce have been recovering from the tragic deaths of so many of their people. As their population grows, they have become stronger as a people and have begun to assert their rights as an independent nation. During the Great Depression, they rejected the Indian Reorganization Act of 1934 which restored some Native American rights. Instead, they adopted their own tribal constitution in 1948. Under this constitution, the Nez Perce are led by a tribal executive committee whose members are elected at large. The committee is responsible for economic growth, protection of the tribe's natural resources, and investment of tribal income.

In recent years, the Nez Perce have been especially concerned about fishing rights in the Columbia River basin. Actively involved in the Columbia River Inter-Tribal Fish Commission, they have worked to restore the salmon and steelhead runs on the rivers of this region. They have also fought to reclaim lands that once belonged to them. In an agreement with the Bonneville Power Administration, which built dams on the Columbia and Snake Rivers, the tribe has secured hunting and fishing rights on 10,000 acres of their ancestral land.

The Nez Perce have also made strides to pass on their unique customs and history. Every summer, descendants of the Wallowa band gather to honor tribal members who lost their lives in the Bear Paw Mountains during the Nez Perce War of 1877. They reverently sing, pray, and smoke pipes. They hold an empty saddle ceremony in

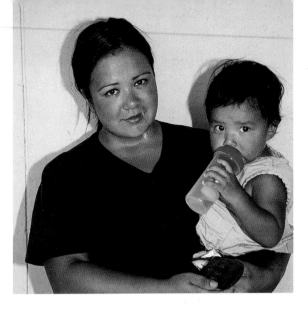

*T*oday, many people raise their families on the reservation, far from big cities, in the Plateau country of north-central Idaho.

which horses without riders are led around in memory of those who lost their lives in this conflict.

In the 1990s, as timber and cattle markets declined, residents of the Wallowa Valley invited the Nez Perce back to the lands where they had once lived for generations. The Nee-Me-Poo Trail, the Nez Perce National Historical Park, and the burial place of Old Chief Joseph have become popular attractions for anyone who wishes to learn more about Nez Perce culture. Residents plan to construct an interpretive center and to purchase 160 acres for the Nez Perce to use for tribal events. Although the initiative has been undertaken to promote tourism, the Nez Perce view the project as a chance to return to the home of their ancestors. As a people, the Nez Perce are working to insure a prosperous future for themselves and their children. As Otis Halfmoon, a Nez Perce, said, "Indian people are still here. We are not going away. It is time that the newcomers to this country started paying proper respect to the elder status of the first nations."

More About

the Nez Perce

Time Line

about 10,000 B.C. Ancestors of the Nez Perce gradually settle in what are now the states of Washington, Oregon, and Idaho.

early 1700s The Nez Perce acquire horses, most likely from the Shoshone, and become expert riders.

1805 The Nez Perce help American explorers Meriwether Lewis and William Clark during their journey to the Pacific Ocean.

1825 French-Canadian fur traders send two Nez Perce boys to the Red River School in Canada.

1831 Four Nez Perce travel 2,000 miles to St. Louis to request teachers for their people.

1836 Henry and Eliza Spalding establish a Christian mission at Lapwai in Nez Perce territory.

1840 Young Joseph, later known as Chief Joseph, is born in the Wallowa Valley.

1840s About 10,000 settlers move through Nez Perce territory on their way to the Willamette Valley in western Oregon.

1855 The Nez Perce agree to a treaty with the U.S. government at the Walla Walla Council that establishes a reservation.

1855–1858 Plateau Indian War is waged.

1861 After gold is discovered, miners pour into Nez Perce country.

1863 At the Lapwai Council, the treaty of 1855 takes away Nez Perce land without the consent of tribal leaders. The new agreement comes to be called the Thief Treaty.

1871 Old Chief Joseph dies and his son, Young Joseph, later known as Chief Joseph, becomes leader of the Wallowa band.

1875 U.S. government opens Nez Perce lands to settlement and subsequently orders tribal members to move onto reservation lands.

1876 At the Lapwai Council, Chief Joseph states that the Nez Perce will not honor the treaty of 1863.

1877 Chief Joseph leads the Wallowa band of the Nez Perce in a desperate attempt to escape to Canada. After a flight of 1,800 miles, the great leader surrenders to the U.S. army and is exiled with his people to Fort Leavenworth, Kansas.

1879 Chief Joseph, now a famous spokesperson for the Nez Perce, travels to Washington, D.C., and requests that his people be allowed to return to Idaho.

1885 Exiled Nez Perce, including Chief Joseph, move to the Colville Reservation in Washington.

1887 The General Allotment Act divides the reservations into parcels that may be held by individuals or sold. The Nez Perce are split between the Nez Perce Reservation in Idaho and the Colville Reservation in Washington.

1893 In the Nez Perce Allotment Agreement, more land is taken from the Nez Perce.

1904 Chief Joseph dies at Colville Reservation on September 21.

1924 Native Americans, including the Nez Perce, are granted full U.S. citizenship under the Snyder Act.

1934 The Indian Reorganization Act acknowledges the right of Native American tribes to form their own governments and practice their own religion. The Nez Perce decide to reject the terms of the act.

1948 The Nez Perce tribe of Idaho establishes an independent government with its own constitution and elected leaders.

1952 The Nez Perce file a claim that they be compensated for lands taken in violation of treaties and for gold mined from their territory.

1959 The Indian Claims Commission awards nearly $20 million to the Nez Perce tribe.

1965 Nez Perce National Historical Park is established in Idaho.

1977 A silver medal bearing the likeness of Chief Joseph is made to commemorate the hundredth anniversary of the Nez Perce War.

1996 The Nez Perce are asked by local officials to return to their ancestral homeland in the Wallowa Valley.

Notable People

Looking Glass (Looking Glass the Younger, Allalimya Takanin) (about 1823–1877), war chief and leader of the Asotin band, was named after his father, who wore a mirror as a pendant. Looking Glass the Younger later received the mirror pendant from his father. At the Lapwai Council of 1863, Looking Glass the Younger rejected the treaty, known later as the Thief Treaty, that took away most of the land of the Nez Perce. However, as did Chief Joseph, he sought to live peacefully with the homesteaders in Idaho. When a military force led by Captain Stephen Whipple attacked his camp on July 1, 1877, Looking Glass decided to join Chief Joseph's group, which had recently skirmished with soldiers at White Bird Canyon. The Nez Perce fought Howard's troops in the Battle of Clearwater on July 11, and Looking Glass became a key war chief in the subsequent flight to Canada. However, he was replaced by Poker Joe after Looking Glass's defeat at Big Hole Valley on August 9. Looking Glass was shot and killed on October 4 during the last battle of the Nez Perce War in the Bear Paw Mountains.

Looking Glass

Joseph (Old Joseph, Tuekakas) (about 1790–1871), leader and father of Young Joseph and Ollikut, was the son of a Cayuse chief and a Nez Perce woman. Achieving renown as a warrior and buffalo hunter, he became chief of the Wallowa band of Lower Nez Perce that made its home in the Wallowa Valley west of the Snake River in what is now northeastern Oregon. Friendly to Americans, he welcomed Henry Spalding, a Presbyterian missionary, and was subsequently baptized as a Christian. He later became a deacon of the church where he was known as Joseph, or Old Joseph.

In 1855, at the invitation of Isaac Stevens, governor of the Washington Territory, he took part in the Walla Walla Council. He joined other Nez Perce leaders in signing a treaty providing for a reservation, but his band kept legal rights to their Wallowa territory. However, when gold was discovered in 1861, settlers poured into the region and officials held the Lapwai Council in 1863. They wished to revise the treaty of 1855 by reducing the reservation from 10,000 to 1,000 square miles in Idaho, including the Wallowa Valley. Old Joseph adamantly refused to sign the agreement. Old Joseph and those who rejected the treaty were called the Nontreaty Nez Perce, while those who signed became known as the Treaty Nez Perce. Rejecting the Euro-American way of life, Old Joseph also destroyed his Bible and American flag.

In a gesture of nonviolent resistance, instead of removing to the reservation he remained on his ancestral land. Over the years, many of the Nontreaty Nez Perce, including Old Joseph, became involved in the Dreamer Faith. Upon his death, his sons Joseph and Ollikut became leaders and fought in the Nez Perce War of 1877.

Joseph (**Chief Joseph, Young Joseph**) (about 1840–1904), famous leader, was born in the Wallowa Valley, the son of Old Joseph and Khapkhaponimi. Baptized as Ephraim, the boy later took the name of his father. Upon the death of his father in 1871, Joseph became peace chief and his brother Ollikut became war chief. Both attempted to maintain their father's practice of nonviolent resistance, but settlers continued to move onto Nez Perce land. In 1875, the U.S. government opened the territory to homesteaders. In a meeting with General Oliver Howard at the Lapwai Council of 1876,

Chief Joseph

Chief Joseph stated that he and his people did not intend to honor the treaty of 1863 in which they had supposedly agreed to give up their ancestral lands. A year later, in May 1877, General Howard demanded that the Nez Perce leave the land on which they had lived for hundreds of years and move onto a reservation near Lapwai, Idaho. When war became inevitable, Chief Joseph unwillingly agreed to surrender the land.

As preparations for the move were underway, however, several young men from the tribe attacked a group of settlers who had previously mistreated them. They killed four of the men and wounded another. Chief Joseph and the rest of his band, including 250 warriors and 500 women and children reluctantly joined the rebels as they fled to Canada where they hoped to find sanctuary. However, about 2,000 U.S. army soldiers pursued the Nez Perce. Over the next four months, the Nez Perce journeyed more than 1,800 miles over mountains, valleys, and rivers in Idaho, Wyoming, and Montana as they eluded the soldiers.

Outnumbered by the better-armed soldiers, the warriors engaged in as many as twenty battles in which they nevertheless skillfully and bravely outfought their opponents. The last battle took place near Sand Creek in the Bear Paw Mountains of Montana—just thirty miles from the Canadian border. For six days, the warriors fought off an army led by Colonel Nelson Miles. Only when General Howard's troops arrived and surrounded them did Chief Joseph finally give up on October 5, 1877.

In addition to his strengths as a leader, Chief Joseph was renowned as an eloquent orator. He gave one of his greatest speeches after the Nez Perce were defeated. Chief Joseph and his band were exiled to Fort Leavenworth, Kansas, and then to Indian Territory in present-day Oklahoma where many of his people died from illness. In 1883, some people were permitted to return to the reservation at Lapwai, Idaho. Two years later, Chief Joseph went to the Colville Reservation with 150 Nez Perce. He was allowed only a brief visit to his home in the Wallowa Valley—despite promises made that he could live there when he had surrendered.

In 1897, he accompanied his former adversaries Howard and Miles on a visit with President William McKinley. In 1903, he and Miles met with President Theodore Roosevelt. Having lost his wife, he married two widows, despite the disapproval of reservation authorities. Upon the death of Chief Joseph in 1904, the doctor on the reservation stated that he died of a broken heart.

Chief Joseph

Hattie Kauffman

Hattie Kauffman (1955–), news correspondent and reporter of Nez Perce and German ancestry, earned a bachelor's degree from the University of Minnesota while working at a Minneapolis radio station. In 1981, she began her career as a professional broadcaster at KING-TV in Seattle, Washington. She became a consumer affairs reporter for *CBS News* in 1990. As news correspondent on *CBS This Morning*, a regular reporter for *48 Hours*, and a feature reporter on *Good Morning America,* she has traveled the world. She has won four Emmies for her work.

Lawyer (Aleiya, Hallalhotsoot) (1796–1876), was the son of Twisted Hair, a leader who welcomed Lewis and Clark into Nez Perce territory, and his Flathead spouse. As a young man, Lawyer worked as a guide and interpreter for explorers and missionaries. He later become a chief of the Upper Nez Perce who made their home on the Clearwater River in present-day Idaho. In 1832, he joined three fur traders, James Bridger, Milton Sublette, and Nathaniel Wyeth, along with their Flathead guide, in their fight against the Gros Ventre in the Battle of Pierre's Hole in Wyoming. In 1838, Lawyer served as an interpreter for the missionary Asa Smith at Kamiah in northern Idaho. Becoming skilled in the English language, he was renowned for his ability as a public speaker.

Along with other Nez Perce leaders, he signed the treaty at the Walla Walla Council of 1855. After soldiers murdered a Nez Perce man named Peopeomoxmox during the Yakima War of 1855–1856, Lawyer protected Governor Isaac Stevens from warriors seeking revenge. As leader of the faction that came to be known as the Treaty Nez Perce, he also signed a treaty at the Lapwai Council of 1863, which drastically reduced Nez Perce territory. In 1868, he went to Washington, D.C., to protest treaty violations. He also wrote many letters expressing his views. He died a year before the Nez Perce War of 1877.

Lawyer

Ollikut (about 1845–1877), son of Old Joseph and brother of Chief Joseph, grew up to distinguish himself as a great hunter and warrior, notably against the Blackfeet and other Plains Indian tribes. When their father died in 1871, Ollikut became war chief of the band while Chief Joseph assumed the role of peace chief. Along with his brother, Ollikut tried to maintain peaceful relations with settlers. However, when conflicts resulted in the Nez Perce War of 1877, he led charges at White Bird Canyon on June 17 and Camas Creek on August 18. He died in the last battle in the Bear Paw Mountains.

Ollikut

Archie Phinney (1903–1949), anthropologist and social activist, was born on the Nez Perce Reservation in Idaho, where he was raised to appreciate the history and culture of his people. An outstanding student, in 1926 he became the first Native American to earn a bachelor's degree from the University of Kansas. He undertook graduate work at George Washington University, New York University, and Columbia University. Returning to the reservation, he dedicated himself to preserving Nez Perce stories. He published *Nez Percé Texts*, a collection of accurate translations with Columbia University Press in 1934. In his work, he demonstrated that folklore was an important field of Native American research. In 1937, he received a graduate degree, the equivalent of a Ph.D, in anthropology from Leningrad University through the Museum of Anthropology and Archaelogy in the former Soviet Union.

He also worked in the federal Bureau of Indian Affairs (BIA) from 1937 until he died in the autumn of 1949. He held several key administrative positions around the United States. At his last post as superintendent on the Nez Perce reservation at Lapwai, Idaho, he was able to provide assistance to many people in the Nez Perce community. In 1943, he was one of the major founders of the National Congress of American Indians and he remained active in this influential intertribal organization for several years. He also lobbied Congress for laws to protect the legal rights and land claims of Native Americans and to support educational programs. In 1946, he received the prestigious Indian Council Fire Award in honor of his work as a scholar and activist. Although he died just three years later, at age 46, his work enabled others to better understand and appreciate the Nez Perce and other native peoples.

Toohoolhoolzote (about 1810–1877), Nez Perce war leader, lived along the Snake River near the mouth of the Salmon River. Along with Old Joseph, he refused to sign the Treaty of 1863 in which the Nez Perce were forced to give up their ancestral lands. He also advocated traditional beliefs among the Nez Perce and took part in a new religion that came to be known as the Dreamer Faith. He was appointed spokesperson of the Lower Nez Perce in 1876, but the following year General Oliver Howard imprisoned Toohoolhoolzote at Lapwai when he would not leave the ancestral territory of the Nez Perce. He was freed when other Nontreaty Nez Perce agreed to terms of the treaty, but conflict quickly led to the Nez Perce War of 1877. Toohoolhoolzote joined with Chief Joseph and played a key role in the victory at Clearwater River on July 11–12. However, on September 30, he was killed in the final battle of the war in the Bear Paw Mountains.

White Bird (**Penpenhihi, Peope Hihhih**) (about 1807–1882), a shaman and leader, refused to sign the treaty of 1863 and relocate to the reservation in Lapwai, Idaho. With Chief Joseph, he sought to live peacefully with the settlers, but when conflicts ensued he allied with Toohoolhoolzote and Ollikut in advocating war. During the Nez Perce War of 1877, he distinguished himself in the Battle of Big Hole Valley in August 9, helping the Nez Perce to escape a large number of soldiers. By the last battle of the war in the Bear Paw Mountains, White Bird and Chief Joseph were the only surviving chiefs. While surrender negotiations were taking place, White Bird, Yellow Wolf, and several other Nez Perce quietly slipped away from the soldiers and escaped to Canada, where they joined the Sioux chief Sitting Bull. When Sitting Bull returned to the United States, White Bird decided to stay in Canada. He was killed by another Indian, angry that the shaman was not able to save the lives of his two sick sons.

Yellow Wolf (1856–1935), warrior and nephew of Chief Joseph, fought in the Nez Perce War of 1877 at the age of 21. During surrender negotiations in the Bear Paw Mountains, he fled to Canada with White Bird and other Nez Perce. They joined the Sioux band led by Sitting Bull. However, the following year, Yellow Wolf returned to the United States with a small band. On their way to the Nez Perce Reservation at Lapwai, Idaho, they were captured and sent to Indian Territory in present-day Oklahoma where

Chief Joseph and other Nez Perce had been relocated after the war. In 1895, some Nez Perce were allowed to return to the Lapwai Reservation, but Yellow Wolf and Chief Joseph were forced to live on the Colville Reservation in Washington. In 1908, Lucullus McWhorter recorded Yellow Wolf's personal history. It was published as *Yellow Wolf: His Own Story* in 1940.

Glossary

allotment A U.S. government policy in which reservations were divided into small, privately owned parcels of land.

Appaloosa A distinctive spotted horse favored by the Nez Perce.

band A group of people loosely bound by family ties, as well as for the sake of protection and the need for food and shelter.

bitterroot A plant with pink flowers gathered by the Nez Perce for food.

breechcloth A strip of buckskin drawn between the legs and tied around the waist.

camas The edible bulb of a wild plant that was a staple of the Nez Perce diet.

couse A plant of the carrot family; the root is boiled or made into dried cakes. Also called biscuitroot.

cradleboard A padded wooden board on which babies were strapped so they could be easily carried.

longhouse Large dwelling covered with bark in which up to thirty Nez Perce families lived.

Nimipu Nez Perce name for themselves, meaning "our people." Also Nimapu.

parfleche A piece of leather folded to form a rectangular pouch and used for storage. From the French word for "rawhide."

reservation Land set aside by the U.S. government for Native Americans.

Sahaptian Language family of the Nez Perce.

sweathouse Small mud-and-grass building used for religious ceremonies.

tipi A conical dwelling made of poles covered with buffalo hides.

Wyakin A guardian spirit who brought good fortune and protected individuals.

Waiyatsit An annual ceremony in which people sang about what they had learned from their guardian spirits.

Further Information

Reading

The following books were consulted while writing *The Nez Perce*. These excellent resources are recommended for anyone who wishes to learn more. The two stories in *The Nez Perce* were adapted from versions published in *Legends of the Nez Perces* as told to Tom Beall by R. D. Leeper and other sources.

Beal, Merrill D. *"I will fight no more forever": Chief Joseph and the Nez Perce War*. Seattle: University of Washington Press, 1977.

Boulé, Mary Null. *Nez Percé People*. Vashon, WA: Merryant Publishers, 1998.

Brown, Mark Herbert. *The Flight of the Nez Perce*. Lincoln: University of Nebraska Press, 1982, 1971.

Encyclopedia of North American Indians. Tarrytown, NY: Marshall Cavendish, 1997.

Gay, E. Jane, Frederick E. Hoxie, and Joan Mark. *With the Nez Perces: Alice Fletcher in the Field, 1889–92*. Lincoln: University of Nebraska Press, 1981.

Haines, Francis. *The Nez Percés: Tribesmen of the Columbia Plateau*. Norman: University of Oklahoma Press, 1982.

Haines, Francis, and Herbert Eugene Bolton. *Nez Percé and Shoshoni Influence on Northwest History*. Berkeley: University of California Press, 1945.

Howard, Helen Addison. *Saga of Chief Joseph*. Lincoln: University of Nebraska Press, 1978.

Howard, Helen Addison, and Dan L. McGrath. *War Chief Joseph*. Lincoln: University of Nebraska Press, 1941.

Johansen, Bruce E., and Donald A. Grinde Jr. *The Encyclopedia of Native American Biography*. New York: Henry Holt and Co., 1997.

Josephy, Alvin M. *The Nez Perce Indians and the Opening of the Northwest.* Boston: Houghton Mifflin, 1997.

Landeen, Dan, and Allen Pinkham. *Salmon and His People: Fish & Fishing in Nez Perce Culture.* Lewiston, ID: Confluence Press, 1999.

Langer, Howard J. ed. *American Indian Quotations.* Westport, CT: Greenwood Pr., 1996.

Lavender, David Sievert. *Let Me Be Free: The Nez Perce Tragedy.* Norman: University of Oklahoma Press, 1999.

McBeth, Kate C. *The Nez Perces Since Lewis and Clark.* Moscow, ID: University of Idaho Press, 1993.

MacDonald, Duncan, and Merle W. Wells. *The Nez Perces: the History of Their Troubles and the Campaign of 1877.* Boise: Idaho Historical Society, 1989.

Malinowski, Sharon. *Notable Native Americans.* Detroit: Gale Research, 1995.

Malinowski, Sharon, and Sheets, Anna. *The Gale Encyclopedia of Native American Tribes.* Detroit: Gale Research, 1998.

Myers, Rex C. *The Settlers and the Nez Perce.* Helena, MT: Montana Historical Society, 1989.

Nez Perce Country: *A Handbook for Nez Perce National Historical Park, Idaho.* Washington, D.C.: U.S. Department of the Interior, 1983.

Nez Perce National Historic Trail: Oregon, Idaho, Montana, Wyoming. Washington, D.C.: Forest Service, National Park Service, Bureau of Land Management, 1994.

Phinney, Archie. *Nez Percé Texts.* New York: Columbia University Press, 1934.

Slickpoo, Allen P. *Nu Mee Poom Tit Wah Tit (Nez Perce Legends).* Lapwai, ID: Nez Perce Tribe of Idaho, 1972.

Slickpoo, Allen P., and Deward E. Walker. *Noon nee-me-poo (We, the Nez Perces): Culture and History of the Nez Perces.* Lapwai. ID: Nez Perce Tribe of Idaho, 1973.

Spinden, Herbert Joseph. *The Nez Percé Indians*. New York: Kraus Reprint Corp., 1964.

Sturtevant, William C., and Deward E. Walker. *Handbook of North American Indians*. Volume 12. Plateau. Washington: Smithsonian Institution, 1998.

Thompson, Scott M. *I Will Tell of My War Story: A Pictorial Account of the Nez Perce War*. Seattle: University of Washington Press, 2000.

Walker, Deward E. *Nez Perce Coyote Tales: the Myth Cycle*. Norman: University of Oklahoma Press, 1994.

Yellow Wolf and Lucullus Virgil McWhorter. *Yellow Wolf: His Own Story*. Caldwell, ID: Caxton, 1940.

Children's Books

The following children's books, several of which were consulted while writing this book, are recommended for young people who would like to learn more about the Nez Perce:

Anderson, Madelyn Klein. *The Nez Perce*. New York: Franklin Watts, 1994.

Davis, Lucile. *Chief Joseph of the Nez Percé: A Photo-Illustrated Biography*. Mankato, MN: Bridgestone Books, 1998.

Garst, Shannon. *Chief Joseph of the Nez Percés*. New York: J. Messner, 1968.

Howes, Kathi. *The Nez Perce*. Vero Beach, FL: Rourke Publications, 1990.

Joseph, A Chief of the Nez Perce. Peterborough, NH: Cobblestone Publishing, 1990.

Lassieur, Allison. *The Nez Percé Tribe*. Mankato, MN: Bridgestone Books, 2000.

Martin, Frances. *Nine Tales of Coyote*. New York: Harper, 1950.

Rifkin, Mark. *The Nez Perce Indians*. New York: Chelsea House, 1994.

Scott, Robert Alan. *Chief Joseph and the Nez Percés*. New York: Facts on File, 1993.

Sneve, Virginia Driving Hawk. *The Nez Perce*. New York: Holiday House, 1994.

Taylor, Marian. *Chief Joseph: Nez Perce Leader*. New York: Chelsea House, 1993.

Trafzer, Clifford E. *The Nez Perce*. New York: Chelsea House, 1992.

Organizations

Nez Perce National Historical Park
P.O. Box 93
Spaulding, ID 83551
(208) 843-2261

The Nez Perce Tribe of Idaho
P.O. Box 365
Lapwai, ID 83540
(208) 843-2253

Wallowa Nez Perce Interpretive Center, Inc.
P.O. Box 15
Wallowa, OR 97885
(541) 886-3101
Fax: (541) 886-3016

Websites

Big Hole National Battlefield
http://www.nps.gov/biho/

Chief Joseph
http://www.rr.gmcs.k12.nm.us/domagala.joseph.htm

Chief Joseph Foundation
http://www.Scenic-Idaho.com/ChiefJosephFoundation/

Chief Joseph, Nez Perce (Nimiputimt)
http://www.indians.org/welker/joseph.htm

Chief Joseph Speaks
http://www.pbs.org/weta/thewest/wpages/wpgs660/jospeak.htm

Historical Nez Perce Archive Photography
http://www.nezperce.com/npphoto1.html

National Historic Trails — Nez Perce National Historic Trail
http://www.gorp.com/gorp/resource/us_trail/nezperce.htm

Nee-Me-Poo National Recreation Trail
http://www.tcfn.org/tctour/parks/NeeMePoo.html

Nee-Mee-Poo (The Nez Perce Tribe of Idaho)
http://www.uidaho.edu/nezperce/neemepoo.htm

Nez Perce Literature
http://www.indians.org/welker/nezperce.htm

Nez Perce National Historical Park
http://www.nps.gov/nepe/

Nez Perce National Historic Trail Foundation
http://www.public.iastate.edu/~sfr/npnhtf/npnhtf.html

The Nez Perce War
http://www.bitterroot.net/usdafs/NezPerceWar.html

Official Nez Perce Tribe Web Site
http://www.nezperce.org/

Spalding-Allen Collection Index
http://www.uidaho.edu/nezperce/archmap.htm

Index

Page numbers for illustrations are in **boldface**.

activists, 115
allotments, 105, 118
ancestors, 18, 104
anthropologists, 115
Appaloosa, **39**, 40–41, **102–103**, 118. *See also* horses

babies, 46, **47**
bands, 28, 30, 44, 118
Battle of Big Hole, 90
Battle of Canyon Creek, 90–92
Battle of Clearwater, 89
Battle of White Bird Canyon, 89
birth, 34, 44–46
body paint, 56–57, 65, 76
Bonneville Power Administration, 100
buffalo, 19, 37–38, **45**, 59

camp, **35**
captives, 76–78, 77–78
ceremonies, 46, 49, 67, **74–75**, 100–101, 118. *See also* dances; marriage
children, **6**, 38, 46–49, **47**, **48**, 80, 90, **98–99**
citizenship, 105
Clark, William. *See* Lewis and Clark
clothing, 19, **20**, 52, 56, 62, **63**, **64**, 65, **66**, **84–85**, 118
coming-of-age, 46, 49, 70
compensation claims, 105
councils, 19, 28, 29, 30, 86–87, 89, 90
Coyote, 11–18, **13**, **16**, 33, 70–71, 80–83
cradleboards, 46, **47**
crafts, 62, **63**, **64**, 65, **66**

dances, 73–78
death, 50–52, **51**
disease, 93–94. *See also* healing
divorce, 50

education, 47, **48**, 104
elders, 28, **29**, 38, 44, 46–47, 50, 80
    Native Americans as, 101
enemies, 19, 22, 52–53, **53**, 54, 76–77, 113

families, 46–48, 49–50, 80, **101**
feasts, 46, 52, 77
feathers, **20**, 56, 57–59
fire, 33
fishing, 25, 30, 57, 67, 100. *See also* salmon legend
food, 24–25, 46, 57–61, **81**, 118
forts, **91**
friends, 19, 21, 52, 53–54, 89
furniture, 33–34
fur trade, 21, 86, 113

gambling, 77
games, 78–80
gathering, 18, 30, 44, 59, 65, 72, 118
General Allotment Act, 105
gold, 87, 105
government, 100

hair, 62–64
healing, 73
history, 104–106
horses, 19, **20**, 36, 38–41, **39**, 52, 53, 56–57, **84–85**, 104. *See also* Appaloosa
racing, 77

housing, 19, **26–27**, 30–36, **31, 32, 35, 36,**
    50, 118
hunting, 19, 24–25, 30, 37, 38–40, 44, **45,**
    48, 54, 57–59, **58,** 72, 100

Indian Reorganization Act, 100, 105
inheritance, 50, 52, 67

jewelry, 52, 62
Joseph, Chief, 87–89, **88, 92,** 93, 100, 104,
    105, 108–111, **109, 111**
    commemorative medal, 106
Joseph, Old Chief, 21, 87, 107–108
journalists, 112
justice, 28

Kauffman, Hattie, 112, **112**

land, **8–9, 10, 13, 16,** 21–25, **22, 24, 58,** 59,
    68–69, 70, **79,** 100–101, 104, 105, 106.
    See also reservations; treaties
language, 18, 28, 94–97, 118
Lawyer, 112–113, **113**
leaders, 19, 28, **29,** 30, 87–88, 89, 90. *See*
    also Joseph, Chief; Joseph, Old Chief;
    Lawyer; Looking Glass; Phinney, Archie;
    Poker Joe; Toohoolhoolzote; White Bird;
    Yellow Wolf
legends, **10,** 10–18, **13, 16,** 33, 70–71, **79,**
    80–83, 115
Lewis and Clark, 21, 86, 104
longhouses, 31–34, **32,** 118
Looking Glass, 89, 107, **107**

marriage, 49–50, 52, 77
medals, 106
medicine bundles, 70
medicine men. *See* shamans
men, 18, 34, **48,** 76, 80. *See also* clothing;
    crafts
migrations, 18, 19. *See also* relocation
Miles, Nelson, 93
missionaries, 21, 86, 104, 113

name(s)
    of Appaloosa, 40–41
    of individuals, 46
    of Nez Perce, 18, 118

Ollikut, 87, 90, 113–115, **114**
organizations, 115, 123

paint, 56–57, 65, 76
parfleches, 38, **61,** 118
Phinney, Archie, 115
pipes, 67, 100
pit houses, 30–31, **31**
Plateau Indian War, 87, 104
Poker Joe, 90
population, 93–94, 100
punishment
    of children, 49
    for crimes, 28

races, 77
recipe, 60–61
religion, **68–69,** 70–76, 116, 118. *See also*
    spirits
relocation, forced, 11, 21, **84–85,** 89, 93,
    104, 110
reservations, 21, 86, 93, **98–99, 101,** 104,
    110, 118
rivers, **8–9,** 11, 23–24, **25,** 100
rock formations, **10,** 10–11, **13, 16,** 18

salmon legend, 80–83, **81**
scalps, 76–78, 89
seasons, 19, 23, 24, 28, 30–31, **42–43,** 44,
    53–54, 57–59, 76
settlers, 21, 86–89, 104
shamans, 28, 46, 70, 71–73, **72, 74–75**
sites
    burial, **51,** 51–52
    dancing, 73
    tourist, 100–101, 105
Sitting Bull, 90, 116, 117
slavery, 78

society, 19, 28–30
Spalding, Henry, 86
spirits, 50, 56, 65, 70, **71,** 76, 118
Stevens, Isaac, 87, 113
storage, 33–34, 38, 59, **61,** 65, 118
storytelling, 44, 47, 70–71, **79,** 80
sun, **42–43,** 70
sweathouses, 34–36, 118

taboos, 34, 44, 49
television personalities, 112
time line, 104–106
tipis, 19, **26–27, 35, 36,** 36–38, 118
tobacco. *See* pipes
Toohoolhoolzote, 116
tools, 33, 37, 52, 65, 67
torture, 78
tourist sites, 100–101, 105
trade, 19, **20,** 36, 40. *See also* fur trade
transportation, 19, **20,** 21, 22–23, 36, 37, 38,
        45, 51, 65, **98–99.** *See also* cradleboards;
        horses

travois, 37, 50–51
treaties, 86–87, 104, 105, 113
Treaty Nez Perce, 113

villages, 28, 30, 44
visions, 49, 70

warfare, 19, 21, 22, 30, 52–57, **53,** 70,
        76–78, **77,** 87
        against U.S., 89–94, **91, 92,** 107, 110
wealth, 38, 49, 50–52
weapons, 52, **54,** 55–56, 67
Websites, 123–124
whistles, 67
White Bird, 90, 93, 116
White Bird Canyon, Battle of, 89
women, 18, 33–34, **36,** 37–38, 49, 57, 59,
        72, 78, 90. *See also* birth; clothing; crafts;
        marriage
wyakin. *See* spirits

Yellow Wolf, 86, 116–117

Raymond Bial

HAS PUBLISHED MORE THAN THIRTY CRITICALLY ACCLAIMED BOOKS OF PHOtographs for children and adults. His photo-essays for children include *Corn Belt Harvest, Amish Home, Frontier Home, Shaker Home, The Underground Railroad, Portrait of a Farm Family, With Needle and Thread: A Book About Quilts, Mist Over the Mountains: Appalachia and Its People, Cajun Home,* and *Where Lincoln Walked.*

He is currently immersed in writing *Lifeways,* a series of books about Native Americans. As with his other work, Bial's deep feeling for his subjects is evident in both the text and illustrations. He travels to tribal cultural centers, photographing homes, artifacts, and surroundings and learning firsthand about the national lifeways of these peoples.

A full-time library director at a small college in Champaign, Illinois, he lives with his wife and three children in nearby Urbana.